W9-ALJ-281

THE RANDOM HOUSE BOOK OF
HOW
THINGS WERE
BUILT

First American edition, 1992

Copyright © 1991 by Grisewood & Dempsey Ltd. All rights reserved
under International and Pan-American Copyright Conventions.
Published in the United States by Random House, Inc., New York.
Originally published in Great Britain by Kingfisher Books, a
Grisewood & Dempsey Company, in 1991.

All rights reserved. No part of this publication may be reproduced,
stored in a retrieval system or transmitted by any means, electronic,
mechanical, photocopying or otherwise, without the prior permission
of the publisher.

Editor: Thomas Keegan
Design: David West Children's Book Design

The publishers would like to thank the following
artists for contributing to this book:

Peter Gregory 20-21, 44-45, 112-113; Terry Gabby (Associated
Freelance Agents Ltd) 16-17, 28-29, 116-117; Stephen Conlin 22-23,
36-37, 40-41, 52-53, 60-61; Kevin Maddison 24-25, 30-33, 38-39, 64-65,
86-89; Chris Lyon 80-81; Sebastian Quigley (Linden Artists) 34-35, 56-
59, 128-131; Dean Entwistle 104-105; Roger Walker (N.E. Middleton)
48-49, 102-103, 110-111, 126-127; Colin Woolf (Linda Rodgers
Associates) 54-55, 96-97; Michael Fisher (The Garden Studio) 62-63,
66-69, 76-77; Frank Nichols (Linda Rodgers Associates) 72-73; Claire
Littlejohn 42-43, 70-71, 74-75, 78-79; Darren Pattenden (The Garden
Studio) 84-85, 92-93, 98-99; Peter Dennis (Linda Rodgers Associates)
90-91, 94-95, 106-107, 108-109, 120-123; Chris Orr 100-101, 118-119,
124-125; Sharon Pallent (Maggie Mundy) 26-27; Gareth Lee (The
Gallery) 14-15, 18-19; Neil Gower (The Organisation) 50-51.

Library of Congress Cataloging in Publication Data
Brown, David J.
The Random House book of how things were built/David J. Brown.
p.   cm.
Includes index.
Summary: An illustrated history of more than sixty notable structures
of the ancient and modern world. Includes detailed diagrams and a
glossary of architectural terms.
ISBN 0–679–82044–2 (trade); ISBN 0–679–92044–7 (lib. bdg.)
1. Architecture—Juvenile literature. [1. Architecture]
I. Title. II. Title: How things were built.
NA2555.B68 1992
720—dc20
91–27638

Manufactured in Hong Kong   10 9 8 7 6 5 4 3 2 1

Note to the reader:

Words set in **bold** type
can be found in the
glossary at the back of the book.

THE RANDOM HOUSE BOOK OF
HOW
THINGS WERE
BUILT

DAVID J. BROWN

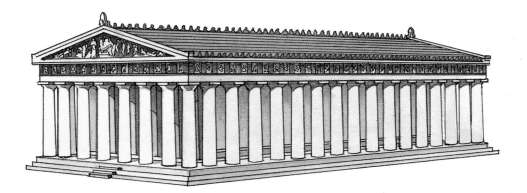

Random House 🏠 New York

CONTENTS

THE ANCIENT WORLD

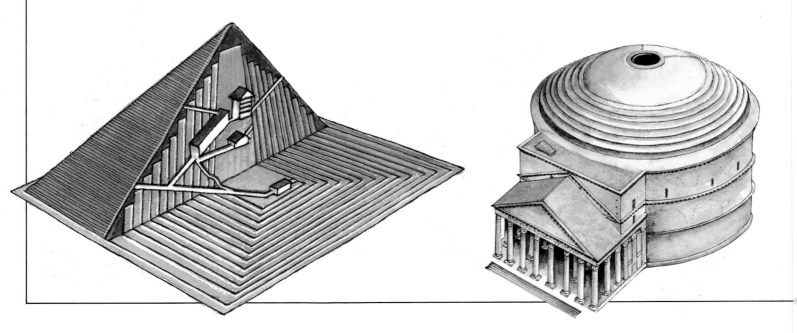

THE AGE OF DISCOVERY

THE "NEW" TECHNOLOGY

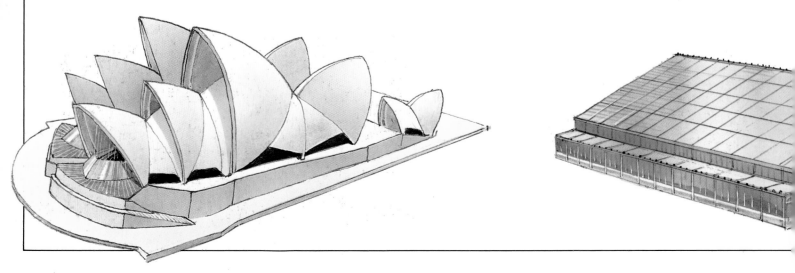

THE MODERN WORLD

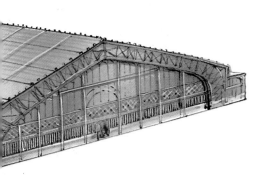

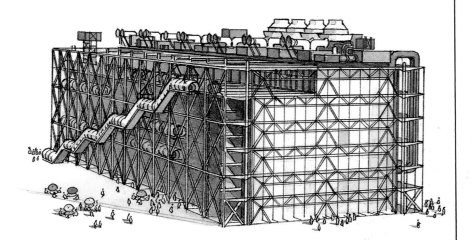

THE ANCIENT WORLD

This book is called *How Things Were Built*, but it might equally be called *How* Were *Things Built?*, for many questions remain unanswered. We start with the very earliest, primitive traces of human habitation and move on to the sophisticated structures of today—and what may come in the future. It is an exciting story, full of monuments. But don't forget that for every monument that has survived, there have been tens of thousands of simple buildings that have vanished. This first section begins with the earliest builders and continues on to the **Gothic** age.

EARLY DWELLINGS

Man has been on Earth for hundreds of thousands, perhaps millions, of years, but the oldest building we know of is only 12,000 years old. The popular image of primitive people has them living in caves. This was often true, but these people must also have built shelters and even more permanent dwellings from which the first settlements grew. In cold lands early hunters built shelters with wooden **frames** and animal skin coverings. Where wood was scarce they used large mammoth bones as supports for their huts. Building a house had great advantages over living in a cave, for in a cave there was no escape from wild animals. Also, rocks often fell from cave roofs, crushing the inhabitants.

CAVE PAINTING

These drawings date from the Upper Paleolithic, or Old Stone Age, period and are about 15,000 to 20,000 years old. They were found in caves in southern France and show what might be huts with central pillars and sloping **rafters**. They would almost certainly have been made from wood, as were the Paleolithic huts built by the mammoth hunters described above.

THE MAIN FRAME

The main supports of the building were made from many reeds tied into bundles and fixed firmly in the ground. They were then bent over and joined at their tips using strips of reed twisted into rope.

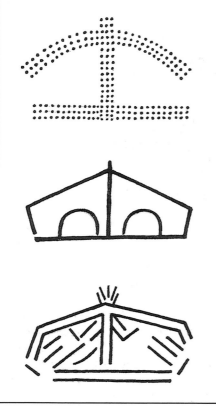

THE FINISHED HUT

Huts, like the one shown on this page, were built in Mesopotamia. There are reports of buildings such as these being more than 60 feet long, 20 feet wide, and up to 10 feet high. Each reed bundle was a yard thick at the base. They were built in areas which were quite warm, and so were well ventilated against the summer heat.

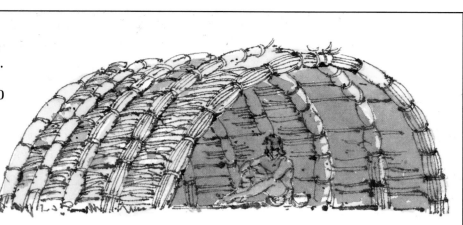

THE COVERING

The finished **arches** were joined with horizontal strips of wood. These supported the final wall material, made from sections of reed matting. This outside wall stopped a yard above the ground. Below that was a loose skirt of matting that could be lifted to cool the interior.

MATERIALS

The huts were made mainly of reeds, picked from the marshes bordering the Tigris and Euphrates rivers in what is now southern Iraq. The reeds were gathered into bundles and tied together using rope made from twisted reeds.

ÇATALHÜYÜK

The battle of Jericho, when the walls of that city were supposed to have come tumbling down, took place around 3400 B.C. There still are walls at Jericho, in Jordan, which are perhaps three times as old as that. Around 10,000 B.C., some peoples in the Middle East began to settle and cultivate crops, the first steps toward civilization in what historians call the Neolithic (New Stone Age) revolution. Abundant fresh water made Jericho a luxuriant oasis, a natural center. Another early city, Çatalhüyük, thrived about 8,000 years ago. Remains show that the people who lived there grew crops and raised cattle, and were also skilled metalworkers, potters, and woodworkers.

TIMBER FRAME
The builders used the simplest materials to build Çatalhüyük. They first built a strong wooden framework of upright posts and horizontal beams. The walls were filled in with rows of **mud bricks**, fixed together with a **mortar** of semi-liquid mud.

Access through roof by wooden ladder

THE WALLS
Once the walls were completed, they were covered with a thick layer of daub, a gooey mixture of mud and straw.

THE BRICKS
The bricks were made from mud which was shaped into the correct size using wooden molds. Once shaped, the bricks were turned out and allowed to dry in the sun. When they were dry, they could be used to build houses.

THE ROOF

The houses in Çatalhüyük were all built next to each other, with no spaces between them. Because of this the town had no streets, so to move from house to house people walked across the rooftops. Instead of having a front door, each house had a hole in the roof. A ladder led down into the main body of the building.

TOWN PLAN

Çatalhüyük, a town in Anatolia, Turkey, was like Jericho. It was a crowded collection of mud-walled flat-roofed houses. Each house was built on the **foundations** of the previous house, giving the town a curious, stepped look.

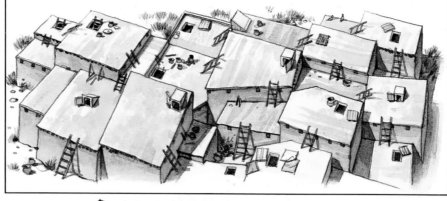

THE INSIDE WALLS

The interior walls were covered with a fine layer of lime plaster. Onto this the people of Çatal-hüyük painted decorations and linear designs in red paint.

TEMPLES

Some houses in the town were given over to religion. These shrines were decorated with pictures of headless figures and huge birds of prey. Animal skulls covered in plaster (to make them as lifelike as possible) were hung from the walls. People were buried in shallow graves.

INSIDE THE HOUSE

The builders made some of the furniture in the house from mud bricks. There were low platforms for sleeping, a higher platform used as a table, and a small oven.

THE FIRST ENGINEERS

From around 3000 B.C., the first city-states arose in what is now the Middle East. You might have seen some of their names—Uruk, Ur, Accad, Babylon, Nineveh. All of them depended upon agriculture, which requires water. In a barren land like this, the principal sources of water were the flood-prone Euphrates and Tigris rivers. From these, complicated networks of irrigation channels had to be built. These channels were fed in turn by main canals that carried water from the rivers.

STEP PYRAMID

Egypt has always been a lush and fertile area, an area of desert fed by the great Nile river. It gave rise to civilizations long before the Pharaohs ruled the land. At first there were two Egypts: Upper Egypt and Lower Egypt. They joined and were ruled by the Pharaohs. Early dynasties rose and fell but very little is now left of their building. The great works of the Third Dynasty appeared in about 2700 B.C. and were the designs and inventions of one man. He was not a Pharaoh, but his chancellor. He was the first man of genius whose name is recorded: an astronomer, writer, philosopher, physician, and most important for this subject, an architect. His name was Imhotep.

IMHOTEP
Imhotep designed and had built the first **pyramid**, the **tomb** of his Pharaoh, Djoser, at a place called Saqqara, near Memphis. This is what it may have looked like.

THE FIRST STAGE
The first thing the builders did was level the ground and mark out the areas that would be taken up by the different layers.

THE SECOND STAGE
The second stage was to build up the central layer to about chest height. Around this the first **buttress** was started, to allow the central core to expand.

THE FINISHED PYRAMID

Imhotep's work at Saqqara did not stop with the step (or buttress) pyramid. It is merely the central feature of a vast complex of tombs and temples enclosed by a wall nearly a mile long, all built in quarried **stone** rather than mud bricks. This meant that the complex was able to survive much longer than earlier mud-built structures.

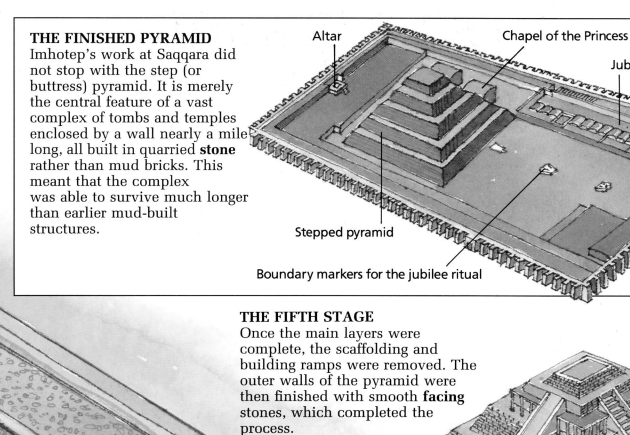

Altar

Chapel of the Princess

Jubilee Court

Stepped pyramid

Boundary markers for the jubilee ritual

THE FIFTH STAGE

Once the main layers were complete, the scaffolding and building ramps were removed. The outer walls of the pyramid were then finished with smooth **facing** stones, which completed the process.

THE FOURTH STAGE

Building ramps and **scaffolding** (*see main picture*) were added to haul the large quantities of bricks and other materials up to where they were needed.

THE THIRD STAGE

Each layer was built up until it was one to two yards above the one below. This continued until the outer buttress was started.

GREAT PYRAMID

During the 100 years after the first pyramid was completed, other pyramids were being built in the same way, with improvements every time. The climax of pyramid building came in about 2550 B.C., when the most colossal of all were erected at Giza, a few miles north of Saqqara. The Great Pyramid, the tomb of Pharaoh Cheops, is 755 feet long on each of its four sides, and stood 479 feet high. (It has lost about 33 feet in height, because its facing stones were robbed for later building material.) The Pyramid of Khafre, still standing close by, is only a little smaller. The Great Pyramid is still one of the largest structures ever built and one of the Seven Wonders of the World.

THE PYRAMIDS AT GIZA
They remain the most colossal funeral monuments ever built. How they were built (they are solid and each weighs over 6,000,000 tons) is one of the greatest riddles of archaeology—and construction. A possible method of the techniques used is illustrated here.

LEVERS
A recent alternative to the ramp theory (opposite page) states that the pyramids were built with skilled teams of men using **levers** only.

TRANSPORT
The Egyptians had to move around 2,000,000 blocks of stone to build the Great Pyramid. They did so without the wheel, so each stone was dragged on sleds over rollers or planks.

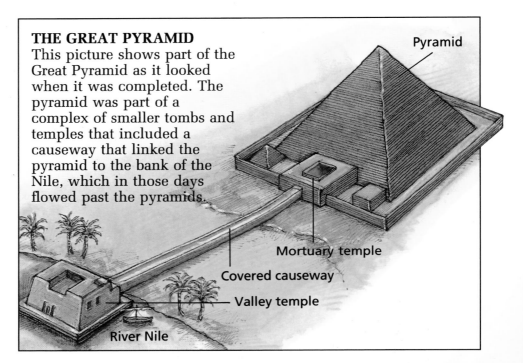

THE GREAT PYRAMID
This picture shows part of the Great Pyramid as it looked when it was completed. The pyramid was part of a complex of smaller tombs and temples that included a causeway that linked the pyramid to the bank of the Nile, which in those days flowed past the pyramids.

Pyramid

Mortuary temple

Covered causeway

Valley temple

River Nile

STAGE ONE
First, the area on which the pyramid was to be built was laid out. The corner stones were placed precisely, then the mass of main blocks were laid out all over the base, and lastly, edge blocks were placed all the way around the outside.

STAGE TWO
The corner blocks of the next layer were levered up by teams of men. Others packed material underneath both the blocks and the levers until they were level with the top of the first course. Then they were pushed into place.

THE INTERIOR

During construction the builders were careful to incorporate tomb chambers and access passages. Before any building took place, the underground tombs were dug out of the bedrock, or solid rock, far below. Workers bashed a tunnel from the rock using hammers made from a hard stone called dolerite. The body of the pyramid contained a network of passageways and burial chambers.

SMOOTHING OFF

Smooth facing blocks were added from the top downward until the builders had achieved a perfect pyramid shape—the largest there has ever been.

STAGE THREE

The course blocks were placed, then the edge blocks, and so on, up and up for 200 courses. It took thousands of men, working in teams, perhaps 20 years to finish.

WERE RAMPS USED?

Most books will tell you that pyramids were erected by slaves pulling 2½ ton **limestone** blocks up vast ramps of earth. To be at an angle shallow enough for the stones to be dragged up, the ramp would have been three times as big as the Great Pyramid! But there is no sign of this ramp material around anywhere.

EGYPTIAN TEMPLES

As engineers, the Egyptians almost equaled the Mesopotamians in their skill at canal building and irrigation. But their building technique did not advance greatly even though they continued to erect buildings of great power, including this temple dedicated to the god Amen at Karnak, completed in 1250 B.C. Although impressive in size, it is very simply constructed.

THE COLUMNS
The tops of **columns** in Egyptian buildings were decorated to look like common plants such as the palm and the papyrus, which reminded Egyptians of the myth that Egypt was the first land to rise from the sea.

GATEWAY
The main entrance to the temple of Amen (*right*) is typical of Egyptian temple building. The two tall towers, or pylons, led through to pillared courtyards and to an inner shrine where a statue of the god stood.

BUILDING A TEMPLE
The Egyptians never learned to span long spaces using **cantilevers**, or arches, so they used simple stone **lintels** across two uprights. The columns were made in sections, stacked on top of each other and decorated (*see below*).

ABU SIMBEL

Of the seven great temples built to Ramses II, an Egyptian Pharaoh, Abu Simbel is the most imposing. Behind the **facade** lies a series of temple rooms. The whole complex was designed so that twice a year the rays of the rising sun shone straight into the entrance. They passed through the great hall, the second hall, the vestibule, and the sanctuary, and finally lit up four statues of the gods.

STONE DRILLING
This illustration of Egyptian stone drilling was found in a tomb of Saqqara, dating from around 2450 B.C. No engineer has yet quite worked out how the drill worked. Can you?

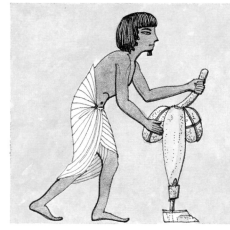

STONEWORK
The Egyptians did not discover a harder metal than copper. This was hard enough for finishing stone, but not for cutting large pieces from the quarry. Large lumps of rock were split by inserting wooden wedges into cracks and then wetting them. The wood expanded, splitting the stone.

ABU SIMBEL
The great figures outside the tomb of Ramses II at Abu Simbel are nearly 100 feet high and all four are of Ramses himself. Behind the facade lies a series of halls and a temple.

MOVING THE TEMPLE
In 1964, the whole temple at Abu Simbel was moved to avoid flooding caused by the new Aswan Dam. The whole structure was dismantled and the statues cut into pieces weighing as much as 30 tons. The temple was then reassembled at a new site.

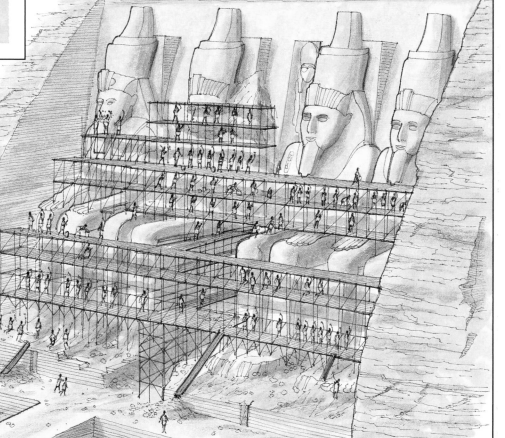

MESOPOTAMIA

The Sumerians, who lived in Mesopotamia, the area between the Tigris and Euphrates rivers (now in Iraq), were the first people to develop and live in cities.

Their houses were constructed from bricks made of clay strengthened with chopped straw; the roofs were made of palm logs laid in rows. As the civilization developed, a type of house evolved which has remained to our day in much of the world: a hollow square with doors and windows facing inward into a shaded courtyard. On the outside, except for the front door, there was a blank brick wall. This shape was the best way to cope with the intense summer heat (and this is still so today).

BARREL VAULTS

This is a **barrel vault** about 5 feet across in a tomb at Ur, 2000 B.C. The curved bricks lean back and inward on each other for support, making this a very strong structure. The wall at the end had to be strengthened to carry the bricks' weight.

FIRED BRICKS

The bricks that were used had a built-in problem (as did the even more basic plain sun-dried mud bricks we read about previously). When it rained, they tended to dissolve.

CONSTRUCTION

The solid mud-brick core of the **ziggurat** at Ur was covered with 8 feet of burnt brick, set in bitumen with layers of matting to make it hold together.

THE HANGING GARDENS

The most spectacular ziggurat of all was the most famous, the Tower of Babel, maybe over 295 feet high, built by King Nebuchadnezzar at Babylon around 600 B.C. You have probably also heard of the Hanging Gardens of Babylon, one of the Seven Wonders of the Ancient World. We can now only guess at what they looked like. Currently, in 1992, the present dictator of Iraq, Saddam Hussein, is building a reconstruction of Babylon on the original site; unfortunately, the irreplaceable remains of the actual ancient city have been destroyed in the process.

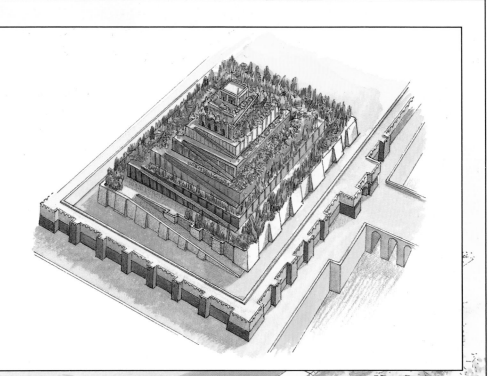

TRANSPORTATION

It is well known that the Mesopotamians had wheeled chariots and wagons, so they probably dragged the mud and burnt bricks to the site on these.

TEMPLES

The earliest temples in Mesopotamia were single rectangular buildings, but later ones were more elaborate. The type that became standard is called a ziggurat, a series of stepped brick platforms a little like Imhotep's stepped pyramid at Saqqara. Mesopotamian bricks, however, even kiln-fired ones, were not so long-lasting as Egyptian natural stone. As a result, time and neglect have worn away the ziggurats so that almost none have survived.

AGAMEMNON'S TOMB

North of Egypt and westward from Mesopotamia, across the Mediterranean, a brilliant civilization flourished on the island of Crete from roughly 2500 B.C. to 1400 B.C. The Minoans (named after the legendary king Minos) had links with Egypt, and the buildings of their great palace at Knossos, discovered less than 100 years ago, have much in common

with some of those of the older culture.

Another culture, farther north at Mycenae, also produced a distinctive building style. On these pages you can see the tomb of Agamemnon, a perfectly preserved example of a beehive tomb. These builders had not invented the arch, but used another technique to make the conical structure shown here.

WATER

The Minoans' main engineering achievement was their clever water supply. Over 3,500 years ago, the people living in the palace at Knossos had piped fresh water to bathrooms and bathtubs, and even used a kind of flushing toilet that some regard as better than anything else before the 19th century.

THE LION GATE (1250 B.C.)

See how the great stones on each side above the lintel that forms the top of the gate slope inward, enclosing the lion sculpture, so that they almost meet above it. Now run your eye down each side. Can you see how the weight of these stones is carried by the **corbeling**, not onto the lintel?

CORBELING

As each course of stone was laid, earth was packed tightly around the outside, between it and the shaft, to relieve the pressure caused by the growing weight of the structure. After it was finished, the corbels were chiseled inside to a smooth dome shape.

MAIN SHAFT

The main shaft of the tomb of Agamemnon is built into a hillside.

THE BURIAL CHAMBER

Here, in the 50-foot diameter tomb of the Mycenean king, we see corbeling in three dimensions. Thirty-three circular courses of stones, each set slightly inward from the one below, were built up, layer by layer.

THE ENTRANCE

The entrance also has a corbeled **portico** above, which meets above the central point. The decoration within the corbel has long since vanished.

THE PARTHENON

The center of Greece was Athens, and perhaps the most famous building there is the Parthenon, the great marble temple on the Acropolis, a rocky hilltop and the religious and cultural center of the city. Early Greek temples had been made of mud bricks on stone bases and roofed with thatch. As they grew in size, rows of timber posts were added, at first down the center and then around the outside as well, to carry the weight of the larger roof. In the **classical** age, the Greeks adapted this form to much larger structures in stone and developed the world's first architectural language for defining the various parts of a building—their proportions and their shapes.

BUILDING THE COLUMNS

The columns could not be erected in single pieces, so they were cut in 10 to 12 sections or drums and ground together to make a perfect fit. The Greek builders did not just pile them on top of each other. They cut square holes in each drum, into which wooden blocks were fitted. These had 2-inch holes drilled in their centers. A wooden plug connected the two pieces securely together.

STRUCTURE

Six-foot iron beams were used in the Parthenon to support the **tympanum**. The Greeks were the first people to use **wrought iron** in building.

GROUND PLAN

Greek architects designed temples to a precise mathematical rule to achieve the pure forms visible today. The rule was that the rectangle could be any width, but the length had to be just over one-sixth greater than the width.

THE PARTHENON
Although the Parthenon looks ordered and regular, the architects used tricks to make it seem even more imposing than it really was. The columns bulge slightly and lean inward a small amount. The ones at the corners are slightly thicker than the others.

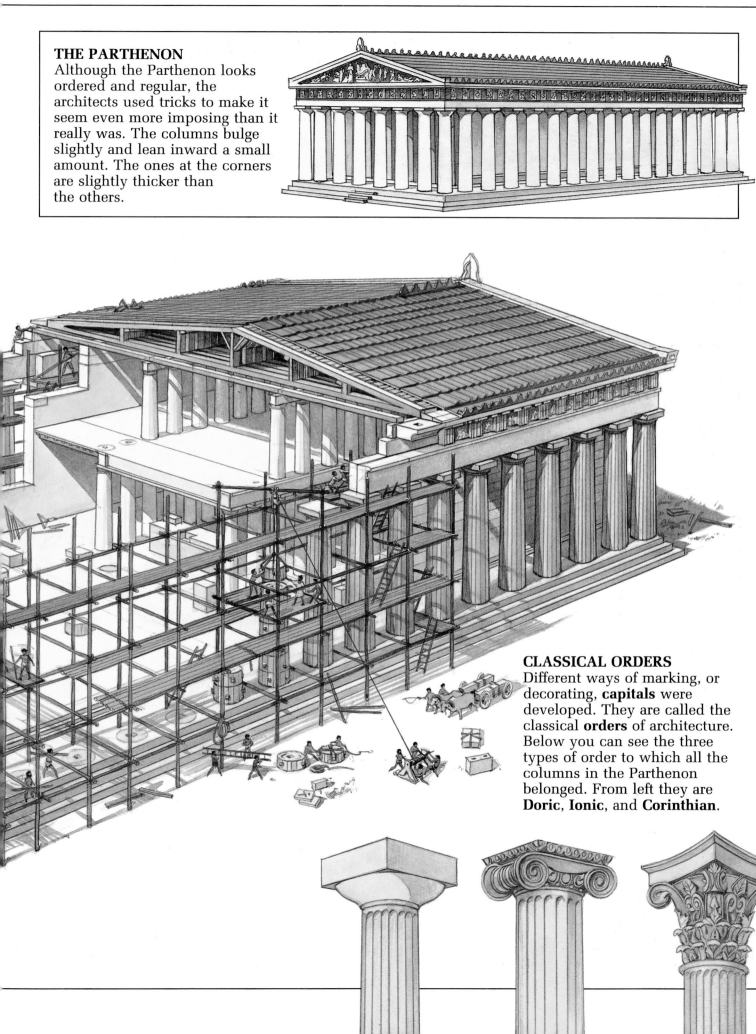

CLASSICAL ORDERS
Different ways of marking, or decorating, **capitals** were developed. They are called the classical **orders** of architecture. Below you can see the three types of order to which all the columns in the Parthenon belonged. From left they are **Doric**, **Ionic**, and **Corinthian**.

THEATER AT EPIDAURUS

The classical age of ancient Greece, famous for advances in learning and culture, was not a time of great progress in engineering.

Temples like the Parthenon, despite the elegance and perfection of their shapes, were not very new in the way they were built. They were really just larger versions of the earlier wooden temples, and their designers and builders do not seem to have been interested in inventing new ways to cross longer distances and thereby enclose larger interiors. The roofs were almost certainly simple timber **beams** and, unlike the durable columns and walls of **marble** and other stone, they have not survived.

GREEK ENGINEERS

The Greeks used their skills to overcome massive engineering problems. The *diolkos*, or slipway, across the Isthmus of Corinth was a 4-mile paved roadway along which ships could be hauled, to avoid the 434-mile voyage around the Peloponnesian peninsula.

THE PLAN

Greek theaters were usually in three parts—the orchestra, where the play was acted; the booth, or *skene*, which housed costumes, props, and sometimes stage machinery; and the *theatron*, a great **terraced** area where the audience sat.

The theatron

Skene

Orchestra

THE STAGE

Many modern buildings use **steel** to add strength. The principle seems to have been invented here, around 500 B.C., though it was not steel, but wrought iron, that was used to strengthen the Propylaea's marble beams. Greek **architects** were skilled craftsmen and usually both designed and built their buildings.

THEATER AT EPIDAURUS

This was built in the fourth century B.C. by the architect Polyclitus the Younger. It can seat as many as 14,000 people, and yet the **acoustics** (sound quality) are so perfect that the smallest sound from the orchestra is perfectly audible everywhere.

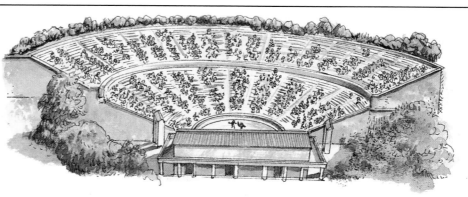

TOOLS

A project to rival modern engineering was a 3,280-foot-long tunnel cut in solid rock and built to carry water from a well in the mountains. Under the direction of Eupalinus of Megara, the first European **civil engineer** known by name, the tunnel was driven from both sides of the mountain. Only a kink of about 16 feet at the joining point shows some error in Eupalinus's calculations.

CONSTRUCTION

The Greeks did not use mortar to hold blocks of stone together. Blocks of stone were joined by molten **lead** poured into grooves and allowed to harden.

THE SIXTH WONDER

The Greek influence on Alexander the Great, king of the Macedonians, was very strong and affected his appreciation of science, language, philosophy, town planning, engineering, **architecture**, and building. Among Alexander's conquests was Egypt. Here he commanded an architect named Dinocrates to lay out a great city, Alexandria, near the mouth of the Nile. Great engineering works were needed to achieve this, including the creation of a harbor by building links between a chain of islands in the sea. The largest of these islands was Pharos, and on this was built the mightiest lighthouse the world has ever seen—the Pharos of Alexandria.

GREEK ENGINEERS

Hellenistic (of the period after Alexander the Great) engineers devised cranes to lift heavy blocks with pulleys that were operated by tread wheels, which were turned by men walking inside them. The engineer Philon was just one of the mechanical wizards of Alexandria. He seems to have invented the bucket chain for raising water, a tremendous step in harnessing the power of nature.

ALEXANDRIA

Alexandria became the center of the Hellenic world. Because it has been continuously occupied since then, little has survived of the original, though it is known that the original layout was based around dividing the city into four areas by two broad avenues crossing at right angles. Under Alexander the Great a great library was founded, tragically destroyed centuries later in a series of fires. Nearby was the museum (the first ancient university), where great scientists worked.

THE PHAROS

Most of the great buildings in this book have survived, at least in ruins, but after being battered by the sea for 1,500 years, the Pharos lighthouse was destroyed by an earthquake in the 13th century A.D. It was one of the Seven Wonders of the Ancient World.

STONEHENGE

Some of the most striking early monuments are standing stones. Over hundreds of sites, these range from single, scarcely recognizable examples, to spectacular rings and other regular arrangements. On these pages you can see the most famous of all, Stonehenge, in southern England. But much more extensive is the great ring at Avebury in Wiltshire, England, so large that it completely encloses a modern village. It is linked by 100 pairs of stones to the man-made Silbury Hill. No one is sure who built this huge conical mound, or why. The purpose of the standing stones themselves is still unknown.

TRANSPORT
The huge blocks of stone were dragged as much as 20 miles using only wooden rollers.

STONEHENGE AND MYCENAE
Stonehenge so closely resembles some of the cyclopean works of Mycenae that many believe there to have been a direct link. Perhaps an exile or traveler from the far-distant Peloponnesus designed and directed the building of this most famous British monument. We shall never know for certain.

The British Isles are full of building remains left by prehistoric peoples—dwellings, forts, temples, tombs—from the Orkney and Shetland Islands north of Scotland to the hills of the south of England.

Sarsens

STONEHENGE

Stonehenge was developed over 1,000 years from primitive Stone Age earthworks to its huge and final form in about 1500 B.C.

— Lintels

MAIN STONES

All the main **sandstone** blocks, weighing 30–40 tons each, were quarried about 20 miles away, dragged to the site, and erected using earth ramps and ropes.

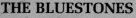

THE JOINTS

Sarsens and lintels were joined by **mortise** and **tenon**, and the lintels by **tongue and groove**. The lintels were shaped on the inside and outside so that the whole outer ring had a continuous curve.

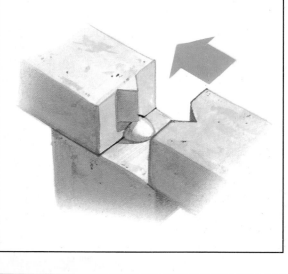

THE BLUESTONES

Within the main monument are a ring and a horseshoe arrangement of bluestones, bluish-gray stones, probably placed earlier and rearranged when the final form took shape. The bluestones were brought by river 150 miles away from a quarry in Preselly, Wales.

LINTELS

Once the upright, or **sarsen**, stones were in place, the lintel blocks were dragged up earth ramps into position.

GREAT WALL OF CHINA

The emperor Tsin Shi Hwang Di became the first ruler of a unified China in the second century B.C. In an almost unimaginably ambitious attempt to unite his great country, he ordered the construction of a wall right across its northern boundary, from the seas in the east to the northwest corner, in order to keep out the nomadic peoples to the north. Several sections of an older wall, built from the seventh century on for the same purpose, were incorporated, but by far the greater portion of the work was new.

The Great Wall covers 1,395 miles, but it has so many loops and branches that the total length could be nearly 4,000 miles.

THE WALLS
Most sections of the Great Wall consisted of a core of earth or rubble faced by tougher material such as stone or bricks and mortar, depending on what was locally available.

PAVING
The roadway along the top was paved with slabs of stone or brick and shielded to the north by a 6-foot high **parapet**; a lower parapet was built on the south, or Chinese, side.

THE TOWERS

The watchtowers are about 30 feet square. In all, there are 25,000 along the length of the wall plus 15,000 others separate from it!

QUARRYING

Of all ancient civilizations, China's had the greatest available range of building materials. From the earliest times, mud bricks, timber, and stone were used, and later **kiln-fired bricks** and tiles, as well.

THE STRUCTURE

The watchtowers are 46 feet high, while the wall itself averages 23 feet. Between 20 and 23 feet wide at the base, it narrows at the top but is still wide enough for a continuous roadway. The wall, when finished, was over 3,700 miles long. In the east much of it still remains in fairly good condition.

Tsin ordered that any workman leaving a crack between the stones large enough to insert a nail should be hanged on the spot.

THE WHEELBARROW

The material used to build the wall was dug by slaves from quarries. Stones being used for the outer walls and the roadway had to be **dressed**, which was done by the local masons. The Chinese invented the wheelbarrow in the third century A.D., which allowed the laborers to work much faster than before.

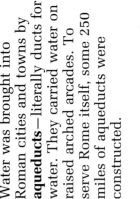

ROMAN ROADS

The Romans built roads because they needed rapid communication between their cities. Roads were the means by which Roman legions could quickly march to quell any rebellion or invasion. Thus, roads had to be both laid out as straight as possible and constructed well enough to withstand the passage of thousands of shod feet marching in time. The first and most famous was called the Via Appia or Appian Way. The Via Appia ran south-east from Rome for over 132 miles. Like many other roads, its line still clearly exists, and in the late 20th century, well over 2,000 years since it was constructed, it now carries traffic over a layer of modern asphalt.

AQUEDUCTS
Water was brought into Roman cities and towns by **aqueducts**—literally ducts for water. They carried water on raised arched arcades. To serve Rome itself, some 250 miles of aqueducts were constructed.

ARCHES
To build an arch the Romans built a light framework to the radius required. Each stone fitted exactly, so no mortar was required.

ROMAN CRANES

The Romans borrowed the idea for this type of crane from a type of Greek hoist (see page 32). They fixed a treadmill to the winding drum, which was turned by one or more people walking on the spot inside the treadmill. The Romans also developed the water wheel and used it to grind corn and to pump water.

BUILDING THE ROADS

Roman roads were built to last. First a trench, three feet or more deep and up to 20 feet wide, was dug. Then a layer of sand was put down, with flat, squared stones in **cement** or mortar placed on top. Next came a layer of gravel in **clay** or **concrete** covered by a layer of sandy concrete, rolled flat. Finally, large blocks of hard rock set in concrete and dressed on their tops formed the roadway itself.

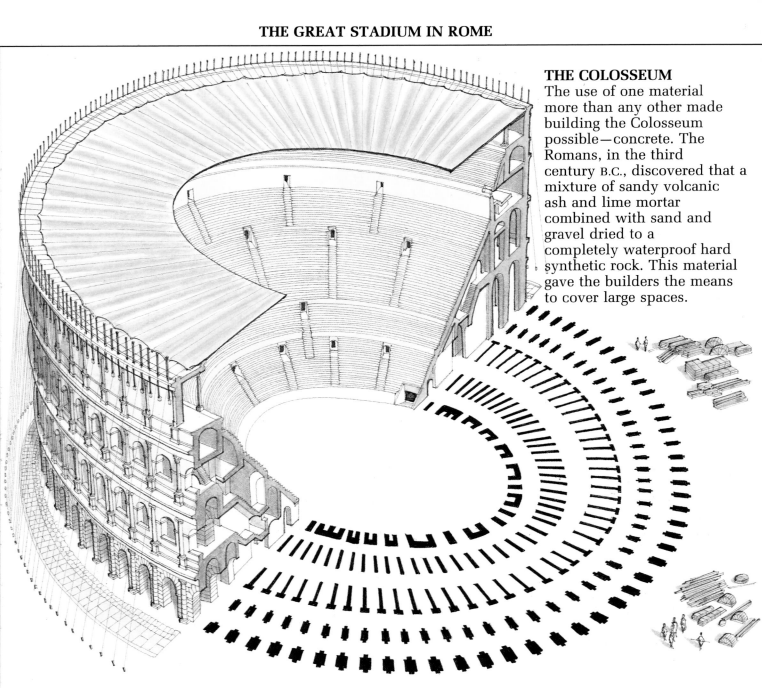

THE COLOSSEUM

The use of one material more than any other made building the Colosseum possible—concrete. The Romans, in the third century B.C., discovered that a mixture of sandy volcanic ash and lime mortar combined with sand and gravel dried to a completely waterproof hard synthetic rock. This material gave the builders the means to cover large spaces.

HOW IT WAS BUILT

The Colosseum was begun by Emperor Vespasian in A.D. 70. Mass concrete was used for the 40-foot deep foundation and brick-faced concrete for most of the vaults.

Building the Colosseum took over 10 years. Beneath the arena was a vast labyrinth of passageways, stores, accommodations for combatants, and dens for the wild beasts.

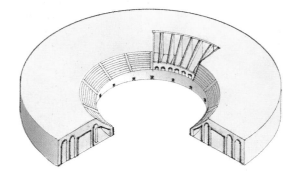

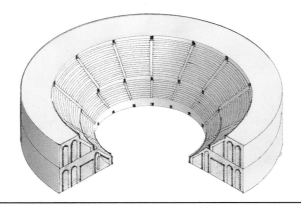

THE COLOSSEUM

The Romans excelled in the creation of huge public spaces and buildings, and successive emperors tried to outdo their predecessors in constructing ever more grandiose monuments: **forums** (open meeting places); **basilicas** (roofed buildings for public assembly); temples (often in imitation of Greek models, with their Doric, Ionic, and Corinthian columns); **circuses** (huge arenas for chariot races—the Circus Maximus was 2,000 feet long and accommodated a quarter of a million people); theaters; public baths; and triumphal arches. Many of these great buildings survive today. These two pages look at one of the Romans' greatest achievements. The Colosseum was built in the first century A.D., and still stands in the center of modern Rome.

VAULTS

The Colosseum, which seated 50,000 spectators for gladiator combats and other spectacles, had three tiers of arched arcades on the outside and a honeycomb of arched, **vaulted** passageways in its vast structure. A vault is simply an arch extended lengthwise, and a semicircular one like the Romans used is a barrel vault. The later Romans discovered that one vault could cross another at right angles and still stand up; this **cross vault** could cover a large square area successfully, supported only at the corners on columns.

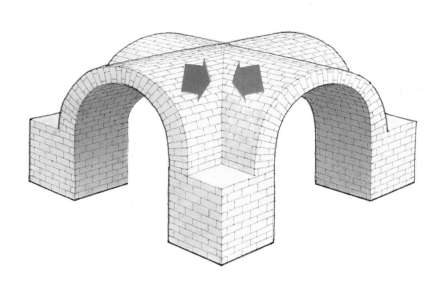

Outside, the first three levels of arcades are faced with Doric, Ionic, and Corinthian columns. Inside, the spectator galleries seated the most important people at the bottom, the least at the top.

The Colosseum was dedicated by Emperor Titus in A.D. 80 with 100 days of games. Two years later Emperor Domitian added the top, Corinthian, story.

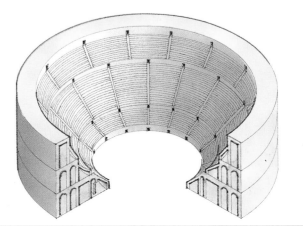

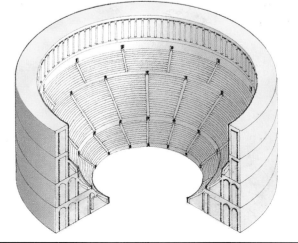

THE PANTHEON

The Pantheon, or Temple of All Gods, was built in Rome by Emperor Hadrian in about A.D. 120. It consists of two parts: a grand entrance, or portico, supported by three lines of 46-foot-high Corinthian columns; and a main building under a vast concrete **dome** 142 feet in diameter. This was by far the largest dome built by the Romans—and hence any people in the ancient world—and remained the world's broadest for 1,300 years. The Pantheon is not important just for its large outside appearance. The intention was to create a huge internal area; the inside is far more important than how the temple looks from the outside. Compare it with the Parthenon, built by the Greeks.

THE WALL
Although the base walls are over 19 feet thick, they contain spaces, or **voids**, some open on the inside. The brick arches carry the weight from above around them and down to the foundation.

STONE WALLS
Several ways were employed to lighten the huge weight of the building (leaving the eye open was one of these). The circular base of the Pantheon has two rings of brick arches built into it which reduced the amount and weight of materials needed to construct the building.

WHAT WAS IT USED FOR?

As with so many ancient buildings, we don't know for certain. It was dedicated to the seven planetary gods, but originally housed statues of Augustus, Agrippa (a Roman statesman), and Julius Caesar, as well as gods and goddesses.

CONCRETE

The Pantheon is the greatest Roman example of the possibilities of concrete. The dome was made of overlapping concrete rings. At the top a circular, brick-ringed hole called an eye was left (big enough to drop a bus through). Without the eye, the dome could not have been built with the materials and techniques known at the time.

The eye

Soffits inside

THE SOFFITS

The dome gets thinner as it rises—from more than 19 feet thick at the bottom to just over 3 feet at the top. Weight is saved by five rings of square hollows, or **soffits**, inside the dome.

EARLY BASILICAS

The largest of the Roman basilicas was built slightly earlier than the Pantheon, by Hadrian's uncle, Trajan, when he was emperor. Only a few columns of its structure now remain, but if you could see it as it was, you would almost certainly be struck by its similarity to the basic form of churches, with a wide central **nave** running its length and two much narrower aisles at the sides. Reality of course is the other way around—the form of the basilicas was the origin of church design. As their shape was such a direct link to this building later seen every day in many towns in the Christian world, basilicas proved to be the most important of Roman building types.

THE ROOFS

A trussed roof—and there is an almost infinite variety of types of truss—is the great alternative to a vault for spanning a large space. The Basilica Ulpia's was most likely of wood, but the portico of the Pantheon originally was supported by a truss of bronze beams.

Pantheon

Teatro Olympico

Notre Dame

13th century church roofs

BASILICA ULPIA

The side aisles of the Basilica Ulpia were almost certainly two-storied, with beams supporting the floor of an upper gallery beneath the timber roof on each side. The central nave, 82 feet wide, would have been roofed by **truss** structure.

Nave

ENTRANCE

Roman basilicas were not always constructed with trussed roofs. The last of them, Emperor Maxentius's Basilica Nova, used barrel vaults instead.

Trussed roof

Aisle

INSIDE OLD ST. PETER'S

Perhaps you have seen the pope on television speaking from the balcony of St. Peter's in Rome. That vast church, the largest in the world, was built between the 16th and 17th centuries on the site of a much older St. Peter's. The illustration on this page shows what that church probably looked like: it had a nave about 82 feet wide with slender walls on Corinthian columns and thicker outer walls that supported a timber trussed roof.

OLD ST. PETER'S

Old St. Peter's survived from the 4th century until it was demolished to make way for the new; the slender inner walls did not have a great deal of strength.

ROOF AND RAFTERS

The wooden roof was quite light in weight, and the long truss beams tied the walls together so that they were not pushed apart.

THE AGE OF DISCOVERY

Many buildings are monuments. They are built to glorify a god or to boast of great wealth or power. Large temples, stadiums, and houses had been built by the Egyptians, Greeks, and Romans, but their methods limited them to a certain size. Without a leap forward, their buildings could not grow. The new architects invented ways to hold up huge domes without obvious support. Churches began to be built with thin supports which held them up from the outside and which allowed them to have thin walls and large windows, which made for vast new spaces. All over the world people were building bigger. This section looks at examples of the great new buildings, including the Gothic cathedrals, a Cambodian temple-city, and a great **mosque** built entirely of mud.

THE HAGIA SOPHIA

This great church was built by the architects Anthemius of Tralles and Isidorus of Miletus in Constantinople (previously Byzantium, now Istanbul) for the emperor Justinian in A.D. 532-537. Some aspects of its design stem from Roman basilicas and concrete dome structures, but much more was new and unprecedented. Even today it is one of the most awe-inspiring buildings in the world.

THE STRUCTURE
Beside the four main piers carrying the pendentives and the dome above, the building has columns of white and green marble which carry galleries and arcades along two sides of the central space.

THE DOME
On top of the curved brick piers the pendentives support a broad, shallow brick dome, the center of which is 200 feet above the floor.

PENDENTIVES
The use of **pendentives** allows the square plan at ground level to carry a dome above. Four vertical supports spread out at the top to form a circle on which the dome sits.

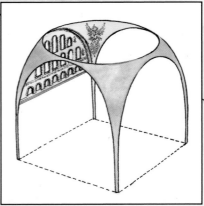

HAGIA SOPHIA

Hagia Sophia was built as a Christian church (the name means Divine Wisdom), and for 900 years it was the principal place of worship in the Byzantine Empire. In 1453, Constantinople was conquered by the Turks, so for nearly five centuries Hagia Sophia functioned as a mosque. In 1935 it became a museum.

INTERIOR

Such an elaborate structure was built just to create the inner space—just as in the case of the Pantheon—though here the shapes seem to float miraculously, so well concealed are the structural means of support.

SMALLER DOMES

More smaller half domes were added farther out and lower down so that from the outside the Hagia Sophia seems like a solid, molded mass of curves, climbing upward and inward to the center.

DURHAM CATHEDRAL

On August 11, 1093, Bishop William of St. Calais laid the first stones in the foundation of the new cathedral at Durham in northern England. It was among the first of all great Gothic cathedrals (although we call it **Romanesque** because the semicircular arches look like Roman ones). Unlike many others, it was built quickly and was nearly complete within 40 years. The walls of the **choir** were erected first, then the **transepts**, then the walls of the nave, and then the vault over the choir—all by A.D. 1100. Within 10 years the transepts were vaulted, and finally the nave.

ROOF

Romanesque churches had been developing for about 300 years. The first stone vaulted roofs covered narrow areas because the slender columns could not carry much weight. Later ones were larger, as the columns became more massive.

ROMAN ARCHES

Yet another technical advance can be seen here: the transverse arches over the nave are pointed, not round. The Gothic Age was under way.

CHANGING PLANS

The cruciform plan gradually began to replace the T-shaped plan of the older Romanesque churches in the 11th century.

VAULTING

At first the vaults were barreled, like Roman ones, and then **groined**. The real structural breakthrough came when strong structural **ribs** were added at the groin.

BUTTRESSES

The transepts at Durham have some of the earliest of these—erected first using temporary wooden **centering**, with the vault **masonry** added afterward between the ribs.

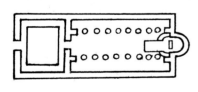

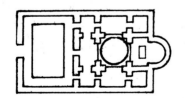

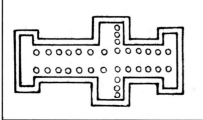

DURHAM CATHEDRAL

A British Sunday magazine supplement had a competition a few years ago to name the best and worst buildings in England. With all the country's architecture to chose from, the readers voted Durham Cathedral as the finest building.

CHOIR

Many Romanesque churches and cathedrals had timber roofs, until they caught fire and were replaced by stone. Durham, however, was vaulted in stone from the outset. The vault built over the choir in A.D. 100 cracked and was replaced in the 13th century.

TRANSEPTS

Medieval churches were decorated in bright colors. Even the columns might have had patterns painted on them. At Durham the patterns were not merely painted but carved into the stonework. The transept pillars have alternate vertical and spiral patterns.

NAVE

The columns in the nave have two patterns: chevrons (lines of zigzags like V's joined together) and diapers (diamonds). The pointed arches over the nave allowed the central ridge to be built in a straight line.

TOWERS

There have always been three towers. The pair at the west end are 144 feet high. The central tower was struck by lightning in 1429 and caught fire. Replacement did not begin for many years, but it was finally restored, in two stages.

CHARTRES CATHEDRAL

In the 12th and 13th centuries, particularly in northern France, cathedral building became a kind of competition between towns. The cathedral at Chartres was begun in A.D. 1195. Other great cathedrals, at Laon, Paris (Notre Dame), Bourges, Reims, Amiens, and Beauvais, were begun around this time. Within 35 years Chartres was nearly finished. Without any of the machinery we take for granted today, a small French town, 800 years ago, had built a cathedral big enough to hold 18,000 people. Many details of how it was built are not known for sure, but it is now thought that Chartres was begun along its entire length and gradually built upward.

PILLARS AND WALLS
Rough blocks of hard, purple-gray limestone were brought from a nearby quarry and shaped in lodges or lean-to workshops against the walls.

FOUNDATIONS
In 1194, the latest of the Chartres churches was burned down, leaving only the towers and the **crypt**. The cathedral we know today was built over the crypt.

Flying buttress

BEGINNINGS
Churches had been built and rebuilt on the same site for centuries before the present cathedral at Chartres was begun.

FLYING BUTTRESSES
In many cathedrals outside support, or buttressing, was needed to stop the walls from being pushed outward. A **flying buttress** connects the wall to a free-standing buttress, lightening the structure.

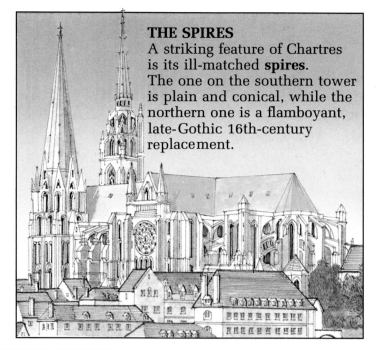

THE SPIRES
A striking feature of Chartres is its ill-matched **spires**. The one on the southern tower is plain and conical, while the northern one is a flamboyant, late-Gothic 16th-century replacement.

WHAT IS THE GOTHIC STYLE?
Arches became pointed, carrying the building's weight much more directly down-ward through thick columns. The walls could now be thinner, often incorporating huge stained-glass windows.

Flying buttress

ACCESS
As the building grew upward, circular staircases, or **vices**, were built inside columns, to allow for further building upward and for fire fighting.

SALISBURY CATHEDRAL

Cathedral design developed very quickly, and in different ways, in England and France. The elegance and lightness of Salisbury, begun in A.D. 1220, is vastly different from both the massive power and weight of Durham and the soaring, elaborate bulk of Chartres. Salisbury's tower, 403 feet high, is the crowning glory.

Work on it did not begin until 50 years after the rest of the cathedral and continued until A.D. 1380. The pointed section of the spire alone is 174 feet tall and octagonal (eight-sided). The design shows great engineering skill—the masonry slabs that form the sides of it are only 9.75 inches thick.

STAINED GLASS

At Salisbury, little medieval stained glass remains, unlike Chartres, which is thought to have the finest in the world. The glassmakers created deep beautiful colors by firing pure white sand with beechwood ash and metallic oxides of various kinds to produce crimson, azure, and other hues.

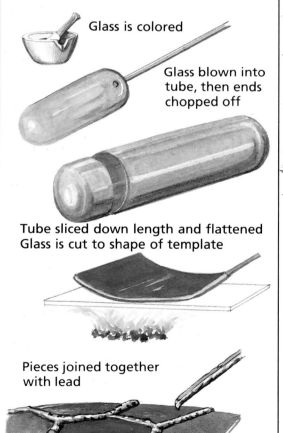

Glass is colored

Glass blown into tube, then ends chopped off

Tube sliced down length and flattened
Glass is cut to shape of template

Pieces joined together with lead

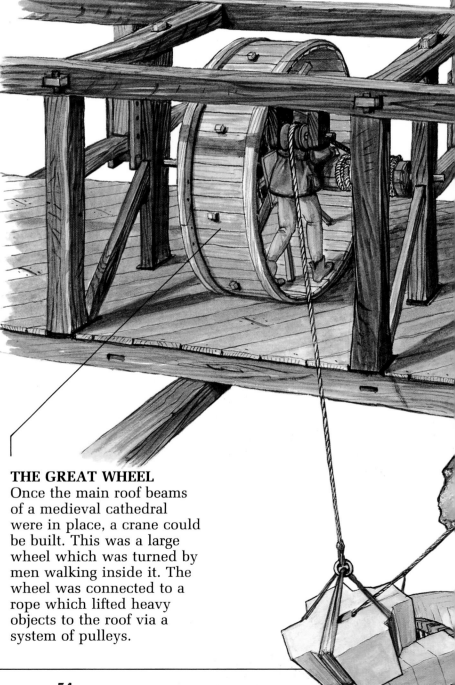

THE GREAT WHEEL

Once the main roof beams of a medieval cathedral were in place, a crane could be built. This was a large wheel which was turned by men walking inside it. The wheel was connected to a rope which lifted heavy objects to the roof via a system of pulleys.

WHO DESIGNED THE CATHEDRALS?

There is no simple answer. Bishops and other churchmen probably contributed to some, as did the Master Masons who supervised the works. In the case of Salisbury, it was probably a man named Elias de Dereham, originally a clerk, and later Master Elias, who also worked at Canterbury and Winchester. The tower and spire, however, were built long after his death.

THE BUILDING

Unlike nearly all cathedrals, no earlier church occupied Salisbury's site. Like Durham it was built quite quickly and is an example of the light, elegant Early English style as is Durham of the heavier Romanesque.

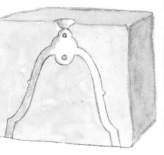

BELLS

Cathedral bells are usually made of bronze—a mixture of copper and tin. They can weigh up to several tons each and are usually sounded by being struck by a clapper.

TOOLS

Most tools, including saws, planes, hammers, and augers, were known to the Romans, but the brace and bit, essential for drilling large holes, was a medieval invention.

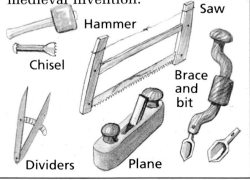

Hammer

Saw

Chisel

Brace and bit

Dividers

Plane

FLORENCE CATHEDRAL

The first great achievement of the Renaissance—the rebirth of learning that followed the Middle Ages or medieval period—was the dome of Florence Cathedral.

The building had been under construction from early in the 14th century, but nothing had been built over the **crossing** because the distance was so vast—138 feet, or as broad as the Pantheon. The architect chosen was Filippo Brunelleschi. Unlike previous large domes, his had one dome inside another to improve weather protection, reduce the total weight, and allow the outer dome to be very tall and imposing.

RIVALRY
At first, Brunelleschi and his great rival, Ghiberti, were jointly appointed to design the dome. Brunelleschi wanted to work on his own, so he pretended to be ill, leaving Ghiberti in charge. Ghiberti couldn't manage alone, so Brunelleschi returned to take over permanently.

HOW WAS IT BUILT?
The inner dome, much thicker than the outer, was built up in rings of large flat bricks, which made it self-supporting. Construction went slowly enough for mortar to set thoroughly at each level before the next was started. Vertical ribs linked the inner shell with the outer, and at three levels chains of stone and **iron** were looped around the dome to withstand forces pushing it outward.

PASSAGEWAYS
Brunelleschi designed passages and stairs between the inner and outer domes to give access to workmen to build both domes from within and to keep them in good repair after completion.

THE LANTERN

When the dome was complete, a competition was held to design the **lantern** to crown it. Brunelleschi had planned for a lantern, and his design was chosen. His lantern has eight buttresses carrying the weight onto the eight ribs of the dome, which in turn direct the thrust down onto the eight piers of the octagonal drum.

THE CRANES

Brunelleschi invented wonderful machines for his building works. An animal-powered hoist at ground level raised and lowered material by rope to scaffolding in the dome, where a man-powered crane raised, swung, and lowered the load onto the work site. On top of the dome (after completion) a crane was installed on rollers for building the lantern. Above this, another crane was installed to complete the cone on top of the lantern.

THE TOWER OF LONDON

The Tower of London is typical of many large medieval castles. It started as a small **motte**-and-**bailey** and was added to over many years. This massive three-story structure stands 92 feet high, with 16-foot-thick walls at the base. The bailey around the tower was at first enclosed by **earthworks** on two sides (this enclosure was called the enceinte) and the existing Roman wall on the others. Another tower, the Bell Tower, was built at the southwest corner of the defenses. By 1250, a bailey around the main building (the White Tower) had been enclosed by a wall with 13 towers. Around this, the existing trench was widened and deepened into a full-fledged **moat**.

TYPES OF CASTLE

When William the Conqueror successfully invaded England in 1066, he built a series of motte-and-bailey castles to establish his rule. The motte was a flat-topped mound of earth with a wooden fortress at its center, the bailey a piece of land for horses and cattle. Timber palisades surrounded both, and for additional protection the motte was enclosed by a trench. Within a few years stone fortresses, or **keeps**, began to replace the wooden ones. Eventually castles became like huge fortified towns, with defenses that could repel attack from any angle.

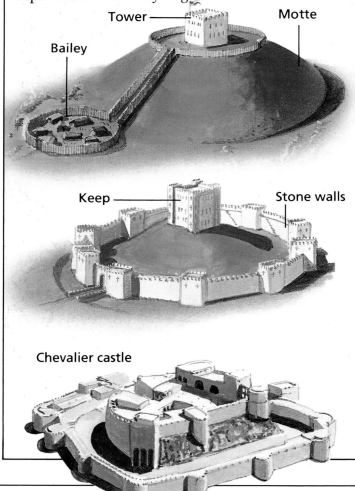

Tower — Motte
Bailey

Keep — Stone walls

Chevalier castle

A.D. 1097
The stone keep of the Tower of London replaced an old motte-and-bailey at the southeast corner of the old Roman wall. It measures 108 feet by 187 feet.

Keep

Trench

White Tower

A.D. 1200
A trench was dug along the Roman wall and the earthworks, then the Bell Tower was built (to the left of the White Tower in the plan).

Roman wall

TOWER OF LONDON

The Norman motte-and-bailey design with its central keep evolved over the next three centuries into a much more elaborate structure, where the wall itself enclosed the main living and working areas of the castle in a ring of massive towers. Caernarvon castle is the most elaborate British example; aspects of these later designs were borrowed from examples in the East built by the Crusaders.

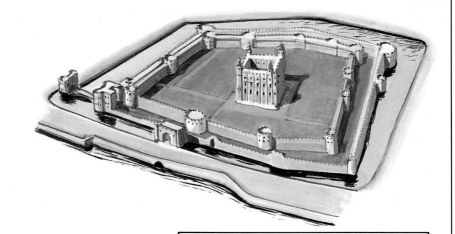

Moat

Stone fortifications on three sides with towers

A.D. 1260
King Henry III converted the tower into a concentric (having a common center) type of fortified castle by his addition of a stone wall with 13 towers.

Western wall added

Wider moat

Traitor's gate

A.D. 1300
After the two concentric stone rings were finished, the river shore was built up and fortified.

THE WHITE TOWER

The keep was always the last defensive refuge in a castle and was usually solidly built. The walls of the Norman White Tower are a sandwich of blocks of stone and marble filling. Buttresses built into the wall shape strengthened the building against attack and its own weight.

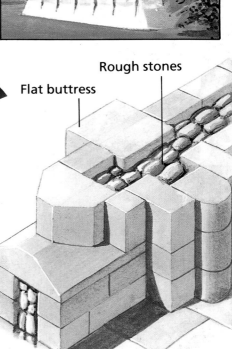

Rough stones

Flat buttress

OLD AMSTERDAM

Some European cities, like Rome and London, called Londinium by the Romans, were founded in ancient times, but others were established much more recently. Amsterdam is special both because it was built on very difficult ground and because of its later development to an elegant, ordered layout. The first building was a keep on one side of the Amstel River, in 1204. Houses grew up around it, spreading to the other side of the river, and in 1342 a defensive ring was built around the town with a moat around it. As the years, and then centuries, went by, and the growing city spread, further rings of ditches were dug and houses built along their banks.

HARBOR

In the 17th century, to accommodate Huguenot refugees who had fled from religious persecution in France, the area of the city was quadrupled in a layout based on four more concentric rings of canals. These were linked by other, radial (like the spokes of a wheel), canals, so that Amsterdam became a city of some 100 man-made islands.

CANALS

The outmost canal, the Singelgracht, is about 6.5 miles long. It was originally surrounded by fortifications, but these were removed about a century ago and replaced with gardens.

MAN-MADE ISLANDS

As a great deal of the Netherlands is below sea level, the Dutch have become very skilled at building on waterlogged land. Amsterdam is an example. It lies on a 50-foot layer of mud on top of 10 feet of sand, and over the centuries has been constructed on thousands of timber **piles**. Many of the islands are made entirely from piles driven into the soft riverbed.

PILE DRIVER

We do not know exactly what type of machinery was used to drive in the original oak piles on which the center of Amsterdam was built, but it probably looked something like this. The driver is mounted in a boat, and the pile is placed vertically between the driver's uprights. A team of men pull a heavy stone weight upward with a rope over a pulley, and let it fall onto the end of the pile. It has been calculated that six or seven volleys of over 20 blows each were necessary to drive a pile down to the proper depth.

MACHU PICCHU

People have inhabited both North and South America for many thousands of years. Both continents contain many impressive monuments, including vast pyramids matching both the height and volume of those in Egypt, though with shallower slopes to their sides.

But perhaps the most impressive of all is the ancient city of Machu Picchu. Forgotten until the early years of this century, it lies high in the Andes Mountains of Peru, 8,000 feet above sea level. It was one of the most spectacular cities in the world, set on a mountainside high above a river valley, in the shadow of a 16,400-foot peak.

LINTELS
Above openings in the walls are simple stone lintels. The stonework here is very like that of the Mycenean civilization—look back at the picture of Agamemnon's tomb.

STONE BLOCKS
Machu Picchu was built by the Incas, whose empire at one time covered large areas of South America. If you were to look closely at the finish of the stonework, you would see precisely cut **granite** blocks that fit together perfectly without the help of mortar.

THE LAYOUT
The city is laid out to a high degree of order, and surrounded by terraces on which were cultivated the crops that sustained the inhabitants.

PUEBLOS

There is far less ancient building in North America than in South America. An exception is the stone dwellings constructed by the Pueblo civilization, sometimes up to five or six stories high, terraced against the cliff in the Canyon de Chelly, Arizona.

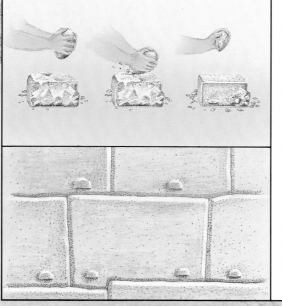

INCA MASONRY

The Incas built the whole of Machu Picchu, a city covering over three square miles, using only the simplest tools. All the buildings are made from large blocks of stone, which fit together with breathtaking accuracy. The blocks of stone were shaped by hand, using very heavy stone hammers. Once the block was the correct shape, it was sanded down to give a smooth finish. One group of houses is called the "ingenious" group because the stones used fit together in such a clever way.

WOODEN BUILDINGS

So far, most of the great buildings in this book have been constructed of stone, brick, or concrete—stacked up, arched over; some mortared, some not. All, though, rely on gravity to hold them together.

A wooden frame is quite different: the various parts—cross, wall, floor, and roof frames—are each made of a number of timbers jointed together and then similarly joined to each other so that the whole structure interlocks in such a way that if it were tipped over, or even forced upside down, it could hold together, provided that the timbers themselves did not break—something that wouldn't happen with a Gothic cathedral or a Greek temple!

OTHER BUILDINGS

We have already seen the use of trusses in roofs, from the portico of the Pantheon onward: some of the most spectacular wooden buildings have very elaborate trussed roofs, like that shown below.

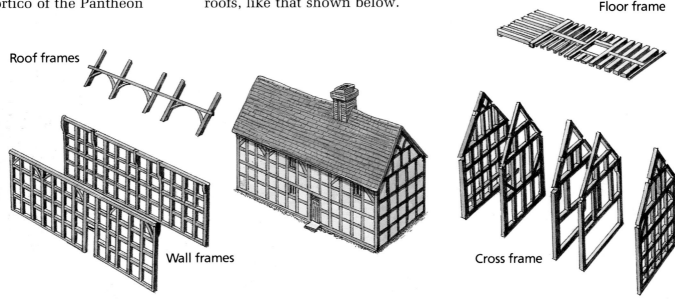

Floor frame

Roof frames

Wall frames

Cross frame

WOODEN JOINTS

In a building resting entirely on a wooden frame, much of the strength relies on the **joints**, the points where the pieces of wood meet and are joined together. Joints have to provide strength and support at points which differ a great deal in the stresses the wood will have to bear. Because of this there are various types, many of which were developed by the earliest carpenters such as the Egyptians, Greeks, and Romans. Many are still in use today, and two of the most common are shown here.

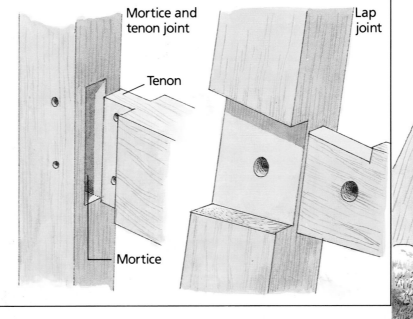

Mortice and tenon joint

Lap joint

Tenon

Mortice

BARNS AND HALLS

Barns usually have three bays, or sections, one for threshing between wide doors and two for storage at each end. The **wattle** walls were often left undaubed for ventilation. Medieval open halls had a large central space, with smoke from the fire having to find its own way out.

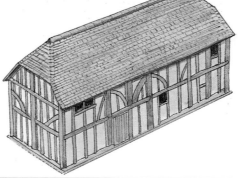

WOODEN FRAMES

Untold thousands of wooden frame buildings still exist in much of the world, dating from the 13th century onward, and including many types of buildings: barns, medieval halls, houses, churches, cottages.

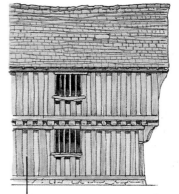

Close studding

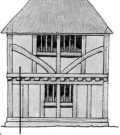

Kentish framing with tension braces

RAISING THE FRAME

Wooden framed buildings were not built **in situ** (on the site), but were **prefabricated** according to a clear plan and then erected frame by frame into the final form.

THE CRUCK

A particularly impressive type of frame is called a **cruck**. To make one, the natural curvature of very large pieces of timber is exploited by splitting the timber in two. The two curved members (the crucks) lean inward to form the main structure.

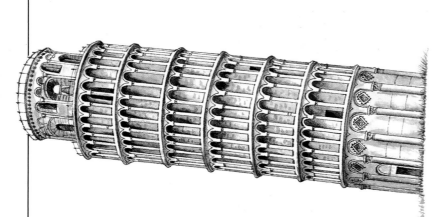

THE LEANING TOWER

In Italy, the bell towers, or campaniles, of cathedrals are often separate from the cathedrals themselves, and that of Pisa is no exception. It was built between 1174 and 1271, with the top bell stage being added in 1350. Almost immediately, it seems, it began to tilt. The tower began to lean even before it was finished. The builders tried to compensate by building the tower so that the top would be straight, even if the bottom half was not. This gave the tower its slightly bent appearance. But the problem was in the ground beneath. It is extremely soft, and the tower's foundations do not spread out over a wide enough area to stop the tower from overloading the ground and sinking.

HOW FAR DOES IT LEAN?

The Leaning Tower has in the last 700 years tilted so far that, over a total height of more than 151 feet and a diameter of 52 feet, it is now 7.8 feet out of true. In other words, if you stood on its topmost parapet and dropped a stone over the edge, it would fall vertically but strike the ground that far from the base.

WILL IT FALL?

The tower is still leaning a little more each year, and the stresses in its stonework are so great that if the movement is not stopped, it will soon collapse.

SAVING THE TOWER

The Leaning Tower is so famous that no one wants it upright again! A method will have to be found to stop the movement, straighten it just a little so that the masonry stresses are manageable, and hold it steady for good.

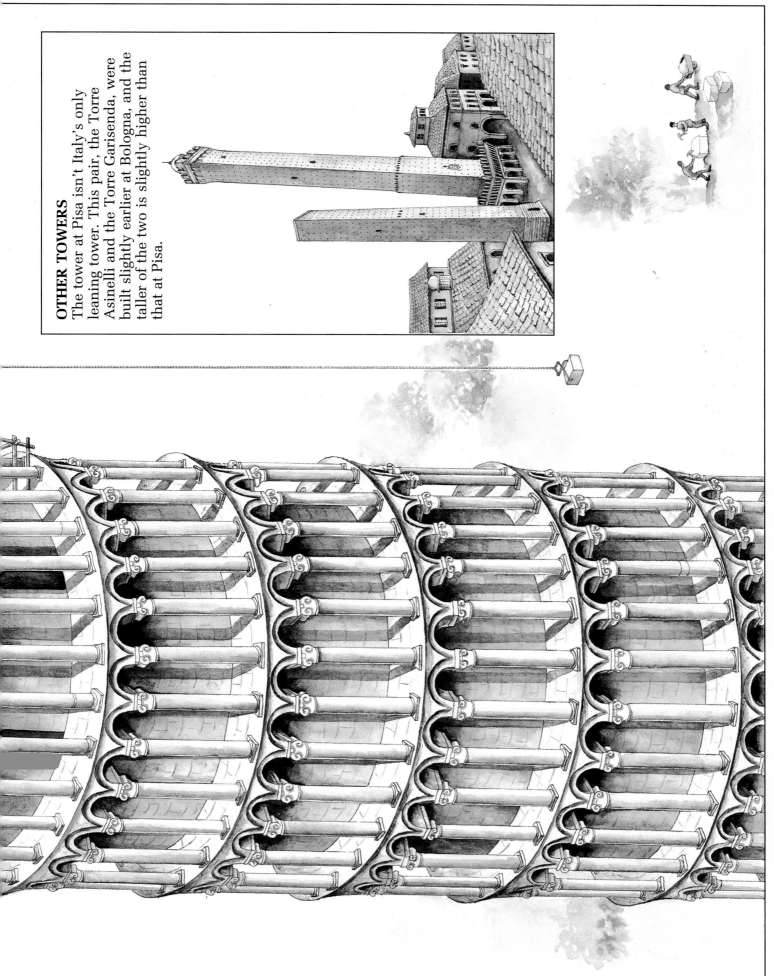

OTHER TOWERS

The tower at Pisa isn't Italy's only leaning tower. This pair, the Torre Asinelli and the Torre Garisenda, were built slightly earlier at Bologna, and the taller of the two is slightly higher than that at Pisa.

WESTMINSTER HALL

On the previous pages we saw that some of the most impressive medieval timber structures were large cruck-framed barns. But the greatest wooden roof of the Middle Ages was neither a barn nor a cruck. In the early 1390s, the English King Richard II commissioned his master carpenter Hugh Herland to design and build in London a great hall for state occasions. The result was Westminster Hall, whose great **hammer beam** roof has remained the largest of its type ever constructed—it has survived nearly 600 years to the present day. Herland managed to span the huge distance of 67 feet without any intervening supports.

Great arch

PREPARING TIMBER

Wooden buildings like those on pages 64 and 65 required large amounts of wood for their construction. This was provided by cutting timber into large pieces shaped like posts and planks.

The first step in preparing timber is to remove the bark. Then it is sliced, using a band saw. Planks are cut many ways to give varying grains. Several ways are shown below.

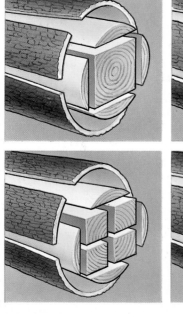

Hammer post

Wall post

HOW IT WAS BUILT

The stone walls were built in the 12th century. Herland's roof was built on them, in 20 days. His only equipment was ropes and pulleys operated by men and horses. Each bay was erected in sections, perhaps beginning with units of wallpost, hammer beam, and arch brace constructed on the ground and lifted onto the walls, forming platforms for further construction.

THE ROOF

The tremendous weight of the roof is shared between the great arch and the hammer posts, then taken down to the stone supports, or corbels, in the walls.

Because the roof is supported halfway down the walls, there is less outward pressure than if the weight were carried along the hammer beams to the top of the wall.

THE HAMMER BEAM

The hammer beams are not in compression (carrying weight) but in **tension**—stopping the rafters from spreading outward. The whole roof supports itself and holds its shape in a wonderful balance of thrusts and counterthrusts, a brilliant structural design which is also a creation of great beauty.

ANGKOR WAT

While the Christian religion in the West attained its greatest and most inspiring architectural expression in the Gothic cathedrals, each reaching toward their heaven in huge vaulted spaces, the Hindu religion in the East found its expression in quite different structures. Throughout southeast Asia elaborately decorated temples survive, and of these none is more awe-inspiring than the Cambodian temple-city of Angkor Wat. Built to honor the Hindu god Vishnu, it shows the Hindu influence in architecture outside India.

BUDDHIST MONUMENTS

If the most characteristic Hindu architectural monument is the temple mountain, that of Buddhism is the **stupa**. These were originally burial mounds, but developed in many varieties of size, shape, and decoration over numerous centuries in India and Sri Lanka. This one, the Ruwanveliseya stupa at Anuradhapura, Sri Lanka, was erected in the second century B.C. and stands 295 feet tall.

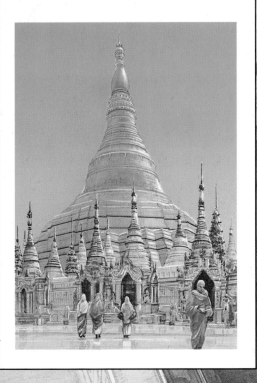

CORBELING

The building techniques included corbeling with wooden beams in the centers of hollowed-out stone blocks for reinforcement. The Khmer's strength lay in grandiose formal layout, and their skill in embellishing every surface with intricate decoration.

CONSTRUCTION

Built in the 12th century A.D. by King Suryavarman II, Angkor Wat is the greatest achievement of the Khmer civilization of Cambodia. It is surrounded by a moat 2.5 miles long and constructed of a combination of brick, sandstone, and laterite, a product of rock decay.

ROOFS

The corbeled vaulting only allows small spaces to be spanned, so each large section of the temple is built of many small units, linked together by galleries.

THE COURTYARDS

The courtyards are covered by corbeled eaves and **pitched roofs**. No mortar was used, but the joints were so finely matched that they are still watertight.

CENTRAL COMPLEX

The central temple complex of Angkor Wat is vast, measuring some 1,150 feet by 820 feet and covering over 86,000 square feet. Within the outer wall is a series of terraces, galleries, and **colonnades** adorned with many towers and pavilions, both at the corners and along the sides, and rising toward a central block. The central block has four towers, one at each corner. The largest of all is in the center, rising to a height of 213 feet. The whole complex forms a beautifully decorated, fantastic mountain of stone.

OLD LONDON BRIDGE

Compared with medieval cathedral design and building, bridge construction in the Middle Ages seems to have been a crude and uncertain process, and few examples survive intact. The most famous was Old London Bridge, but despite the fact that it lasted 600 years, it seems to have been a lesson in how not to build bridges. Begun in 1176 by a man named Peter of Colechurch to replace an earlier wooden bridge, it was not completed until 1209. Even though long spans had been achieved in other countries, London Bridge had 19 arches over its 650-foot length, plus a drawbridge section for security, all built upon **starlings** (*see below*).

THE PIERS

Gradually, during the 33 years of the bridge's construction, **coffer-dams** were staked out across the river, one after another, outward from the banks, and oak and elm piles were driven inside to provide foundations for the piers. From barges moored against the stream, rocks were piled into the coffers, then planks laid on top as a base. The lowest was placed at low tide.

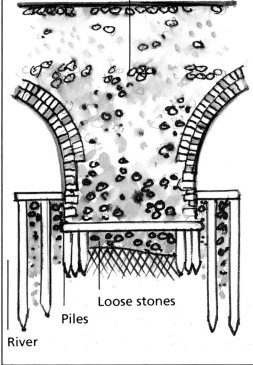

Ashlar masonry on outer wall, loose stones inside

Loose stones

Piles

River

PRESSURE ON FOUNDATIONS

The piers were prone to erosion, so the history of London Bridge was one long saga of endless repairs. This was made worse by the fact that all kinds of buildings—houses, stores, inns, even towers—were built on top, along its length.

STARLINGS

The starlings, built in the water to protect the piers, and the arches were not only of different sizes and distances apart, but their total width filled two thirds of the distance across the Thames River. This meant that the already fast flow was fiercely concentrated in certain places.

HOUSES

The houses were both naturally unstable (a whole row once fell off into the river), and also brought greater pressure to bear on the foundations. This brought great problems in maintenance.

NEW BRIDGES

London Bridge the second was built in 1831. It was taken down in the 1960s and bought by an American town (Lake Havasu City, Arizona) and re-erected as a tourist attraction. The new bridge is of **reinforced concrete**.

THE TAJ MAHAL

Perhaps the most famous building in the world, and one which has been called the most perfect, is this great marble **mausoleum** built to house the body of an Indian empress by her grieving husband.

The Mogul emperor Shah Jahan began its construction, near the city of Agra, in 1630, the year after the death of his wife Mumtaz Mahal. Over 20,000 workmen took 11 years to complete the mausoleum itself, and a further 11 for the surrounding wall, mosques, gateway, and **minarets**. The perfect proportions, intricate decorations, and pure-white marble surface belie the size of the Taj Mahal and the massiveness of its structure.

BRICKWORK

At the building's four corners stand what are, in effect, the main parts of the structure: four octagonal towers with small domes on each summit. The inside faces of these are linked so that together they carry a central inner dome, 80 feet high and 58 feet in diameter, above the tomb of the empress.

Though pictures can give the impression that the Taj Mahal is more like a sculpture than a building, it is, in fact, taller than the great Hagia Sophia in Istanbul.

THE TOMB

The central chamber of the Taj Mahal is octagonal. In the center are marble monuments (called cenotaphs) dedicated to Shah Jahan and his wife. They are surrounded by fantastically delicate carved marble screens inlaid with precious stones. Beneath the chamber, in a vault sunken within the podium on which the visible bulk of the building stands, are the sarcophagi, or stone coffins, containing the two bodies.

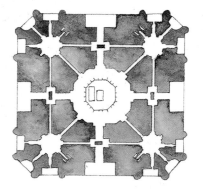

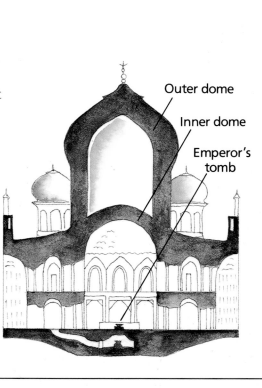

Outer dome

Inner dome

Emperor's tomb

THE LAYOUT

The whole complex measures 1,903 feet by 997 feet, and within this the Taj Mahal itself is 614 square feet in plan. On each of its four identical facades an arch rises to a height of 108 feet.

THE DOME

The feature which caps the whole design and completes the world-famous profile of the buildings is the second, or outer, dome in the center. Its outer wall curves outward in the characteristic slightly bulbous East Indian fashion before curving inward to its topmost point, nearly 200 feet above the floor of the building.

ST. PAUL'S CATHEDRAL

One of the casualties of the great fire of London in 1666 was old St. Paul's, the largest Gothic cathedral in England. A single architect, Sir Christopher Wren, designed and supervised the building of the new St. Paul's between 1675 and 1710. Its design combines several features we have already encountered: Romanesque semi-circular arches inside, classical columns and capitals on the facades, Gothic flying buttresses concealed behind them, and **baroque** decoration on the ceilings. But the most original part of the design is concealed from view—the structure of the great dome. Compare its structure to the Pantheon and the Duomo in Florence.

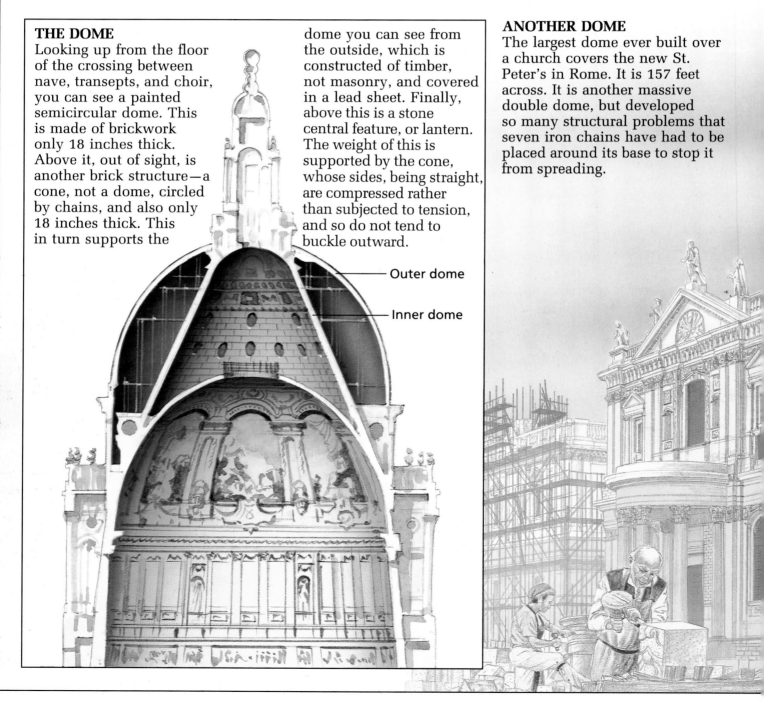

THE DOME

Looking up from the floor of the crossing between nave, transepts, and choir, you can see a painted semicircular dome. This is made of brickwork only 18 inches thick. Above it, out of sight, is another brick structure—a cone, not a dome, circled by chains, and also only 18 inches thick. This in turn supports the dome you can see from the outside, which is constructed of timber, not masonry, and covered in a lead sheet. Finally, above this is a stone central feature, or lantern. The weight of this is supported by the cone, whose sides, being straight, are compressed rather than subjected to tension, and so do not tend to buckle outward.

— Outer dome

— Inner dome

ANOTHER DOME

The largest dome ever built over a church covers the new St. Peter's in Rome. It is 157 feet across. It is another massive double dome, but developed so many structural problems that seven iron chains have had to be placed around its base to stop it from spreading.

WREN'S DESIGN
Wren's masterly design, far lighter and more stable than any before, spans 102 feet and rises 366 feet above ground level to the tip of the cross, with four sections.

Wren was born in 1632. St. Paul's was his greatest and most influential work, but his hugely productive 91-year life also included 51 other churches in London and throughout England, the Sheldonian theater in Oxford, the partial rebuilding of Hampton Court Palace, and Greenwich Royal Hospital for sailors.

THE ROYAL CRESCENT

The Romans built a city called Aquae Sulis on the site of present-day Bath, England. The baths still survive, fed by natural springs thought to have health-giving properties. Although Bath maintained prosperity through trade for centuries, it never lost its reputation as a health resort, and in the 18th century it became highly fashionable to "take the waters," an act which was supposed to cure many common ailments. Two local architects, John Wood and then his son, John Wood the Younger, progressively designed a new city layout of grand formality. Fortunately, the perfect building material lay near at hand, the honey-colored local limestone known as Bath stone.

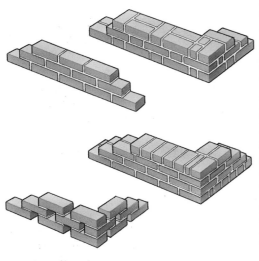

BRICKS

There are many different ways of using bricks to build a house. A feature of bricklaying is that bricks are never laid so that the vertical joints lie above each other. Bricks laid with the narrow end facing out are called headers. Those with their long side showing are called stretchers. Bricks are laid in patterns called bonds. The four bonds most commonly used are shown here. Clockwise, from the top, they are English, American, Flemish, and running bond.

FIREPLACES

In 18th-century England, coal became widely burned in fires instead of wood. Fireplaces became smaller. Rather than putting a large pile of wood way back under a large chimney, with a lot of heat escaping up it, coal was put in an iron basket-like grate and set forward in a smaller fireplace. This heated the room more efficiently.

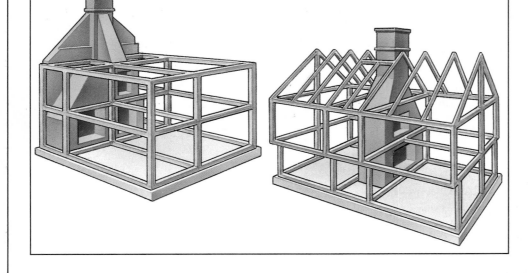

ROYAL CRESCENT

The Royal Crescent is a vast but simple semicircle of 30 houses facing down a hillside in Bath. It has the grandeur of a palace, almost an English Versailles, but was built as housing for ordinary people, not for a single all-powerful ruler.

BATH STONE

Use of Bath stone in construction was a local feature, but the layout of the Woods' designs at Bath was copied all over England: continuous terraces designed as an architectural whole turned the cost of land into a design benefit. Standard **load-bearing** brick walls carried the weight of floors and roofs, with wooden **joists** spanning between interior walls.

JOHN WOOD

John Wood's first big development in Bath was Queen Square (1729). More than 50 years later, after a vast amount of further building, his son produced the greatest glory of Bath, Royal Crescent.

THE MOSQUE AT DJENNE

Some building techniques, though outdated, are still in use because the technique used suited a particular area well. Today, nearly half the world's population live in mud structures, and as thoughts turn to environmental conservation, the low cost and simplicity of this medium is increasingly attractive. At Djénné, in Mali, West Africa, earth construction has become a highly sophisticated art. Masons have a long and detailed training (in guilds, similar to Western practice, from medieval times onward). They have constructed some of the most elaborate earth buildings in existence, including the world's largest—the Great Mosque.

BUILDING TECHNIQUES

To create internal spaces, and to support the mud roofs, wooden ceilings are laid in an ingenious crisscross pattern so that nowhere are timbers the entire width of the roof.

The timber-mud roof is heavy, and so needs thick walls to support it. This doesn't matter, however; mud is plentiful, and the thicker the walls the better they insulate the inside against both the cold-season night and the hot-season day.

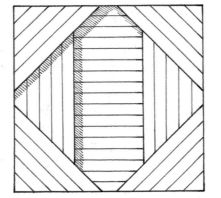

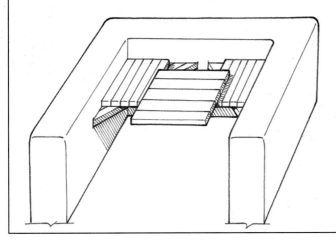

STYLE SOUDONNAIS

This strange, decorative type of architecture is known as the style Soudonnais, or Sudan style. It has heavy walls and small window openings due to the climate, but the highly ornamental, organic, molded appearance makes the buildings look as if they have grown—which in a sense they have.

GUTTERS

To get rain off the flat roofs, gutter pipes of fired clay are placed around the edges. These stop water from coming down the sides of the building and washing them away.

MOLDED

The Great Mosque was completed in 1907. Although some mud building is erected by the molding of whole walls in molds (**pisé de terre**), the Djénnénke masons use **adobe** (mud bricks). These are laid to make walls of either 23-inch thickness (for two stories) or 16-inch thickness (for single stories).

OUTER SKIN

The great problem with mud construction is that rain can easily wash it away. To make the outside walls rain resistant, rice or millet hulls are mixed into the adobe.

THE "NEW" TECHNOLOGY

Once buildings made of stone reach a certain size, they begin to collapse under their own weight. Structures made of iron or steel can grow to enormous heights—or, in the case of bridges, they can span very long distances. Some of the buildings looked at so far have used metal as one form of support, but it was not until the Industrial Revolution in the 18th century that enough iron was available to even consider making whole buildings from this material. This "new" technology allowed builders to realize their dream of crossing great distances and of building as high as they could. The buildings shown in this section, such as the Eiffel Tower, the Golden Gate Bridge, and the Sydney Opera House, are all structures that are the result of a great vision made possible by the coming of the new iron age.

IRONBRIDGE

The Industrial Revolution—the transformation of the world through the development of steam power and mechanization—grew from one place: Coalbrookdale, in Shropshire, England. There the first blast furnaces smelted iron ore in the 18th century. The **cast-iron** industry developed there rapidly, culminating in the decision to build a bridge, the Ironbridge, across the Severn River. The world's first iron rails were already being cast at Coalbrookdale, so the decision to use cast iron to build the bridge was a natural one. At this point the river runs through a steep gorge, so a high single arch with a 98-foot span was needed.

THE IRONBRIDGE
The Ironbridge rapidly became the first great indicator of the structural possibilities of iron. Can you see the difference between the bridge and stone or brick structures?

MAIN RIBS
The main iron structure was completed in 1778, with the bridge and approach roads being opened in 1781.

STONE ABUTMENTS
Stone abutments were built on both sides in 1778 to carry the approach road. In the following July the first two main ribs, each weighing nearly six tons, were lowered into place.

JOINTS

Iron has so much **tensile strength** that this kind of delicate **lattice** can provide ample support for a large span. It is interesting, though, that at a closer level techniques from other traditions can be seen. For instance, look at the joints: mortise and tenons just as if the ribs and radial **members** were made of wood. This technique was used to construct many timber buildings, including the barns and early houses looked at previously.

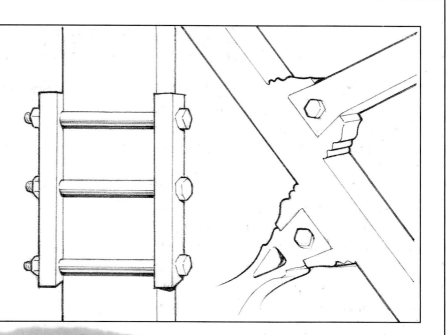

CAST IRON

Although this bridge structure looks more delicate than that of a stone bridge, its 418 tons of iron are far more than is necessary. Its builders seem to have not yet fully understood the enormous strength of cast iron.

MENAI STRAITS BRIDGE

Even when the Ironbridge was built, it was by no means the longest span yet. And within a few years—notably in the United States—wooden and stone bridges three times its length were erected. When the Scottish engineer Thomas Telford approached the task of bridging the 820-foot breadth of the Menai Straits in Wales, he first thought of a cast-iron arch. This would have been far too large for whole half-span sections to be lifted into place by block and tackle, as had been the two halves of the Ironbridge. He planned instead to build out a framework, or centering, from each shore, held back by cables. In the long run, however, he turned to another principle—suspension.

BRUNEL

The greatest 19th-century British engineer was Isambard Kingdom Brunel, who designed railways, tunnels, ships, wooden buildings and viaducts, and brick and masonry arch bridges, as well as two other types of bridges. The Saltash railway bridge (1853–56) has the deck slung from two huge wrought-iron tubes, each over 16 feet in diameter and 453 feet long. The Clifton Suspension Bridge, completed in 1864, spans 709 feet, compared to the 587 feet bridged by the Menai Straits Suspension Bridge.

CENTRAL SECTIONS

Each of the long central sections was floated out in turn on a barge and winched up into place by 150 men pulling ropes around capstans, or rotating vertical drums. A wooden roadway was hung from this structure by thin iron rods. The bridge took six and a half years to finish, and was opened in 1826.

MAIN TOWERS

Stone-arch side supports and two main towers each 148 feet high were built at the sides of the channel, leaving a central span of 580 feet. Sixteen chain cables were needed. Each consisted of 10-foot-long wrought-iron bars bolted together, five abreast, for strength.

SUSPENSION BRIDGE

Primitive walkways suspended from ropes have spanned rivers since before history, and by the 17th century more permanent suspension-type bridges had been designed. In the early 1800s, an American judge named James Finley put principle into practice by designing a **suspension bridge** which crossed Jacob's Creek in western Pennsylvania.

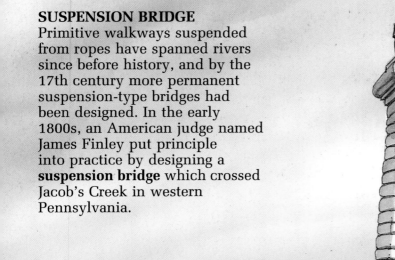

CRYSTAL PALACE

In the late 1840s, a great exhibition of arts and industry was organized by England's Prince Albert, Queen Victoria's husband. A vast building was planned in London's Hyde Park, but the official design was so ugly that a great protest ensued. With only 10 months to go before the planned opening date of May 1, 1851, matters looked desperate.

But after just a week's planning, the architect Sir Joseph Paxton produced an alternative—a colossal glass house to be framed entirely in iron parts. Nothing like it had ever been erected before. It was dubbed the Crystal Palace by a magazine, and though the Exhibition committee resisted this name, the public adopted it.

PREFABRICATION

Every part was designed to be made in sections at plants in Birmingham, brought to London by railway, and assembled in Hyde Park: 3,300 main supporting columns, over 2,000 principal **girders**, thousands of feet of lumber for joists and flooring, and 300,000 square feet of plate glass.

THE RIBS

The whole building was put together in 22 weeks. It was 1,847 feet long, 410 feet wide, and 62 feet high, except where a semicircular barrel-roofed transept, which enclosed large elm trees, rose to 108 feet high.

GIRDERS

There were miles of **guttering** and other components, right down to staircases, lavatories, and a ventilation system which allowed fresh air in at ground level, drawn in by warm air escaping through vents above.

Prefabricated units arranged by horse and cart

CRYSTAL PALACE

It was originally intended that the Crystal Palace would exist for only six months, but when the Great Exhibition closed, it was moved to a site at Sydenham, Surrey, outside London. Much altered and enlarged, it became the home of exhibitions, concerts, firework displays, and much more, until it burned down in 1936. The area on which it stood still bears its name.

TRANSEPTS

Many feared that the building would not be structurally stable, because it was made of such slender and apparently flimsy elements. To overcome this, Paxton cunningly varied the thickness and strength of the members according to the loads and stresses they would have to bear.

GALERIE DES MACHINES

The dome the Romans built on the Pantheon remained one of the world's largest until the middle of the 19th century. The new capabilities of iron and steel allowed designers to leave the ancient standard far behind. In 1869, the great arched station of St. Pancras terminus in London leaped an unprecedented 239 feet, but only 20 years later, its wrought-iron trusses were exceeded by the steel ones of the Galerie des Machines, built for the 1889 Paris Exposition. Steel, a compound of iron and carbon, is of great hardness and has much more tensile strength than wrought or cast iron. It enabled the trusses of the Galerie des Machines to span 374 feet.

PINS
The pins are deliberately included to allow for movement up or down if the metal of the arches expands or contracts, or if the ground supports move slightly.

FEET
There are two further pins in each of the Galerie des Machines' arches. They are out of sight, beneath those precarious-looking triangular feet, connecting them with the mass concrete foundations which stop the arches from spreading outward.

ARCHES
The arches are continuous, and supported on massive brick piers. In the later, larger structure, the tops of the arches are pinned, or held together by joints. These are called **pinned joints**.

ST. PANCRAS
At St. Pancras Station in London, the spreading was coped with by having each side of the arches' feet tied across to the other, out of sight, beneath the railway tracks. Any visitor to London today can still see St. Pancras Station. But sadly, the even more spectacular and innovative Galerie des Machines (the first to use the three-pinned arch) was demolished in 1910.

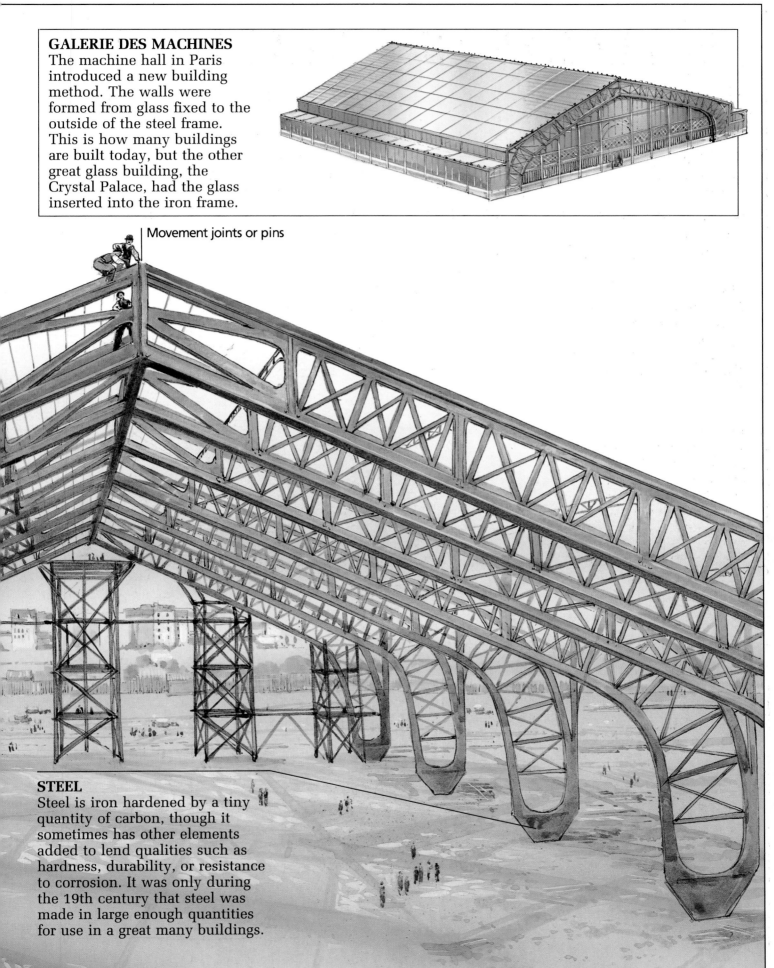

GALERIE DES MACHINES
The machine hall in Paris introduced a new building method. The walls were formed from glass fixed to the outside of the steel frame. This is how many buildings are built today, but the other great glass building, the Crystal Palace, had the glass inserted into the iron frame.

Movement joints or pins

STEEL
Steel is iron hardened by a tiny quantity of carbon, though it sometimes has other elements added to lend qualities such as hardness, durability, or resistance to corrosion. It was only during the 19th century that steel was made in large enough quantities for use in a great many buildings.

FORTH RAIL BRIDGE

Carrying railways across long spans was a huge and new challenge to 19th-century engineers; a long, heavy, fast-moving train caused far greater stresses on a structure than any horse-drawn vehicle or any number of pedestrians. Telford's Menai Straits Suspension Bridge carried a simple road, but when the engineer Robert Stephenson was faced with the challenge of carrying a railway over the same straits, he ran his trains through huge rigid iron tubes. To extend the ever-growing railway system into Scotland, two broad estuaries, or water passages, had to be bridged, the Firth of Tay and the Firth of Forth. The Tay was spanned first, with 85 simple crisscross trusses on brick piers.

STEEL

The Tay Bridge used between 4,000 and 5,000 tons of iron; the Forth needed 58,000 tons of steel. At three times the water depth, multiple brick piers were out of the question, but there was an island midstream near which a central support could be built.

CAISSONS

First to be sited were three huge **caissons**, sunk 88 feet into the river, then filled with concrete to form a base for each tower. The main columns of the towers were next, and gradually the cantilevers were built up and out, stretching out farther and farther until the two halves of each of the two supported spans met and were connected.

STEEL TUBES

This wide stance was a safety device to withstand stresses from high winds; another was to make all the main members from steel tubes, to better cope with compression forces (the widest are 13 feet across, big enough to drive a train through).

SUPPORT

To bridge the Forth an engineer named Sir Benjamin Baker proposed a cantilever bridge. His design was for the biggest bridge in the world—two clear spans of nearly 1,706 feet each; three colossal cantilevering support towers, 1,348 feet long, 328 feet high, and 120 feet wide at the bases.

CANTILEVERING

The principle of cantilevering is that of a rigid bracket or arm extending out from a support to carry a load. As applied to bridge engineering—and the Forth Bridge is the greatest and most famous example—rigid, braced trusses extend outward from supports to carry a span.

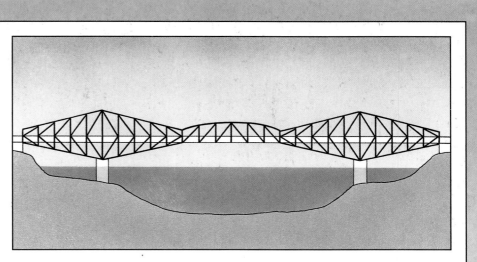

FORTH BRIDGE

The Forth Bridge was completed in 1889; ever since then, it has been continuously painted. By the time the workers have reached one end the other needs to be painted, and they have to start all over again. Structurally it is as stable as the day it opened.

THE TAY BRIDGE

The Tay Bridge's middle 13 girders were not adequately connected with the others, and on December 29, 1879, they collapsed in a gale, taking a mail train with them into the night waters of the Tay; 75 perished.

THE EIFFEL TOWER

Ever since the mythical Tower of Babel (probably a Babylonian ziggurat), people have aspired to build high. The greatest medieval embodiment of this was the Gothic cathedral. But with the Industrial Revolution came an age which expressed itself in the engineering of commerce—railways, ships, bridges, canals, and exhibitions. Yet perhaps the most striking visual image of all was a tower. It was a celebration of revolution, built in the style and material of the age. The 1889 Paris Exposition celebrated the centenary of the French Revolution, and for this the great tower of iron that has become Paris's famous symbol was erected.

GARABIT VIADUCT

Alexandre Gustave Eiffel designed the 541-foot lattice-arch span of the Garabit Viaduct in 1884. In 1885, the French Ministry announced a competition to design a large tower. Eiffel's 990-foot-tall iron tower won.

FIRST STAGE

The four legs grew upward and inward, supported by wooden scaffolding. Cranes inside the framework of the legs lifted the material for the first floor, which by March 1888 was spanning between and linking up the legs.

PREFABRICATION

Like the Crystal Palace, all the tower's 12,000 pieces were prefabricated off site and assembled with precision down to the last fraction of an inch.

FOUNDATIONS

Once foundation caissons were finished, in June 1887, work on the tower began immediately.

Falsework

March 1888

November 1887

THE EIFFEL TOWER
Despite criticism about its impact on Paris, the tower proved a great popular success in the 1889 exhibition. Eiffel placed a meteorology station at the top in 1889, and in 1901 probably saved it from demolition by using it as a site for radio transmitters.

SECOND STAGE
By July 1888, the second floor, 427 feet high, had been completed. And still the structure climbed. By April 1889, it was complete, held together by no fewer than two-and-a-half million **rivets**.

TOP OF THE TOWER
Many worried at the time that the tower would be felled by high winds, but the combination of widely splayed legs and open-lattice construction, which allows wind to pass through, has ensured that Eiffel's design remains stable in the severest gales.

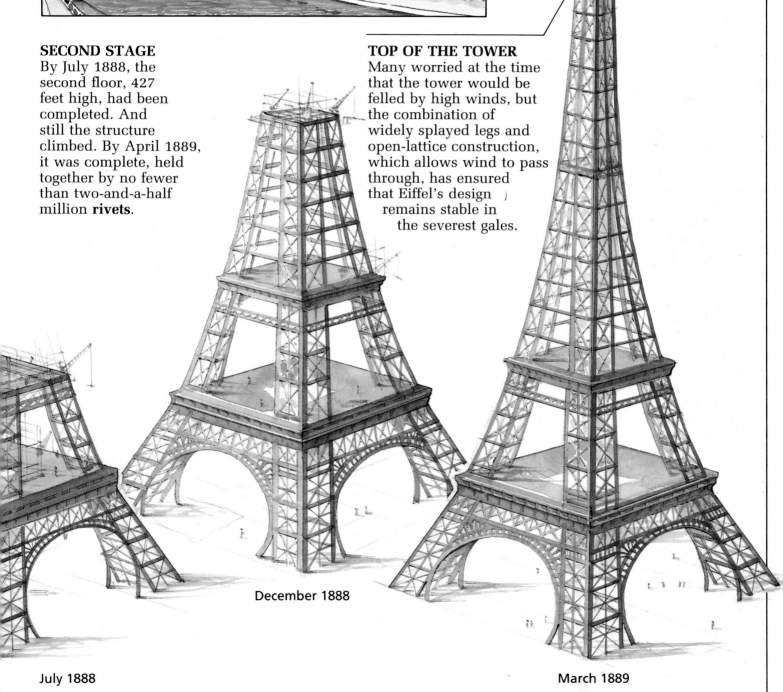

December 1888

July 1888

March 1889

THE SAGRADA FAMILIA

In Barcelona, Spain, a cathedral has been under construction for over 100 years, and is still not even halfway complete. Its very continuation is an act of faith from generation to generation. That it continues to be built at all is a tribute to the extraordinary influence of its designer, Antoni Gaudí, and the

amazing quality of the architecture itself. The Sagrada Familia really has far more in common with the medieval Gothic cathedrals than does any more literal present-day copy. Its design was evolved continuously by Gaudí as he worked on it, from 1884 until his death in 1926.

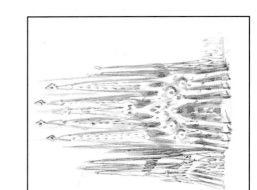

GAUDÍ

In the center, above the 328-foot-long nave, Gaudí planned a cluster of taller towers around a central one, representing Christ and rising to 558 feet. Gaudí's buildings have a strange, organic life of their own, as if they have grown rather than been built. They are made up of rounded shapes, sinuous curves, and bright colors—no straight lines or gray concrete. But Gaudí was a brilliant structural designer as well as a fantastic artist.

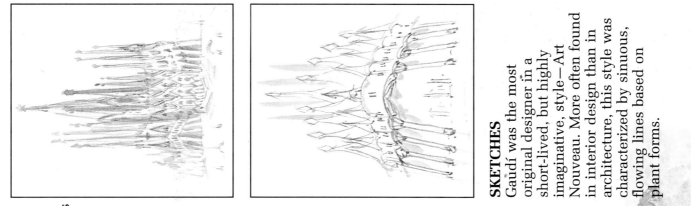

SKETCHES

Gaudí was the most original designer in a short-lived, but highly imaginative, style—Art Nouveau. More often found in interior design than in architecture, this style was characterized by sinuous, flowing lines based on plant forms.

By using hanging chain models to represent the elements of the building upside down, Gaudí realized his own logical extension of Gothic design: tall, slender columns leaning inward like stone forests; supporting vaults neither circular nor pointed but parabolic (the curve becoming tighter near the top). When our descendants finally stand in the completed Sagrada Familia, they will behold the most imaginative, and truest, descendant of the anonymous genius of Chartres.

FACADES

Gaudí envisaged the cathedral as having three facades, each dominated by four 328-foot-high towers; these represent the 12 apostles. At Gaudí's death only one facade was complete—the opposite one was finished as recently as 1985.

EARLY SKYSCRAPERS

We usually use the word **skyscraper** to mean many-storied buildings in which people live and work. These could not have been built until a new method of construction was developed. You may recall how the Crystal Palace gained its strength from a rigid frame. A next logical step seemed to be to erect a rigid frame upward, story by story, and hang walls and floors from it. In 1860, a naval boat store that was built at Sheerness, in Essex, England, developed the principle in an important way. Unlike the Crystal Palace, it had to be built without cross bracing because the boats had to be moved around. So the joints between girders were made to provide thorough support.

EARLY FRAMES

Framed skyscrapers soon exceeded by far anything possible with load-bearing walls. The tallest load-bearing building was the Pulitzer Building in New York, which needed masonry 10 feet thick at the base to carry its 14 stories.

FIRST SKYSCRAPER

The world's first true skyscraper, though it had only 10 stories, was Chicago's Home Insurance Building (1885). It had self-supporting brick walls, but its floors were supported on iron-and-steel frames. Almost immediately, the Tacoma Building, also in Chicago, was put up. It was taller than the Home Insurance Building and almost all its mass, including the brick walls, was supported by the frame.

WHY SKYSCRAPERS?

After the Great Chicago Fire devastated the city in 1871, a building boom followed that raised the price of land. Building high was the best way to get value. William Le Baron Jenney developed the high-rise steel frame, which allowed for buildings taller than ever before.

NAVAL BOAT STORE

The structure of the store is of cast-iron columns, 13 feet off the ground, which support 23-foot-long wrought-iron beams and 13-foot-long cast-iron cross beams. All have an I- or H-shaped cross section and brackets that support the points where they interlock, forming a completely rigid iron frame. Almost certainly, the Sheerness Naval Boat Store was the world's first multistory building with a rigid portal frame, and was thus the direct forerunner of the modern skyscraper.

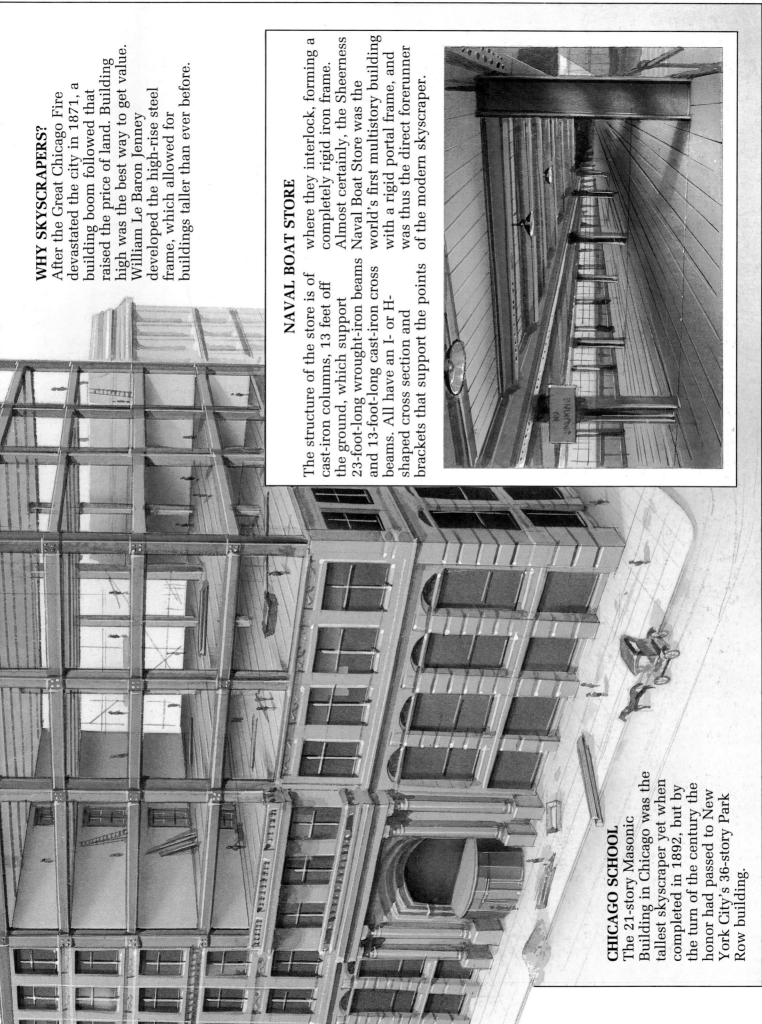

CHICAGO SCHOOL

The 21-story Masonic Building in Chicago was the tallest skyscraper yet when completed in 1892, but by the turn of the century the honor had passed to New York City's 36-story Park Row building.

EMPIRE STATE BUILDING

Up and up went the skyscrapers: the Singer Building, 45 stories, 612 feet; the Woolworth Building, 60 stories, 792 feet; 40 Wall Tower, 71 stories, 927 feet; the Chrysler Building, 77 stories, 1,046 feet. Finally came the most famous of all, New York's Empire State Building, 102 stories, 1,250 feet tall. The first step was to excavate for its foundations: over 700,000 cubic feet of rock and earth were removed to make a hole 56 feet deep. While this was being done, a fast and continuous delivery system for the vast number of steel **H-beams** and **I-beams** was set up. This skyscraper was to remain the world's tallest for the next 40 years.

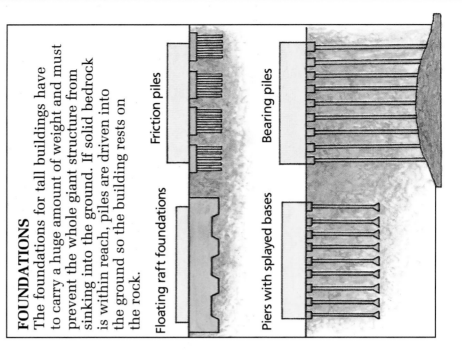

FOUNDATIONS

The foundations for tall buildings have to carry a huge amount of weight and must prevent the whole giant structure from sinking into the ground. If solid bedrock is within reach, piles are driven into the ground so the building rests on the rock.

Floating raft foundations

Friction piles

Piers with splayed bases

Bearing piles

FIRST STAGE

As soon as excavation was complete, erection began. Nine derricks and electric freight elevators lifted the members up through the rapidly growing skeleton of the building.

THE SKELETON

While the upper floors of the steel structure were bolted and riveted together, hundreds of workers poured concrete, fitted windows, placed limestone facings, laid bricks, and installed elevators in the lower floors. In one 10-day period, the building jumped 14 floors. And in an amazing 18-months' time, the entire structure was completed.

ELEVATORS

The development of the passenger elevator meant that tall buildings could get even taller. Elevators are powered by electric motors which wind the main cables up and down. The weight of the elevator is balanced by a counterweight, and in an emergency, such as the cable snapping, the emergency brake grips the side rail and slows the car to a standstill. The first elevator with a safety brake was invented by Elisha Otis in 1854.

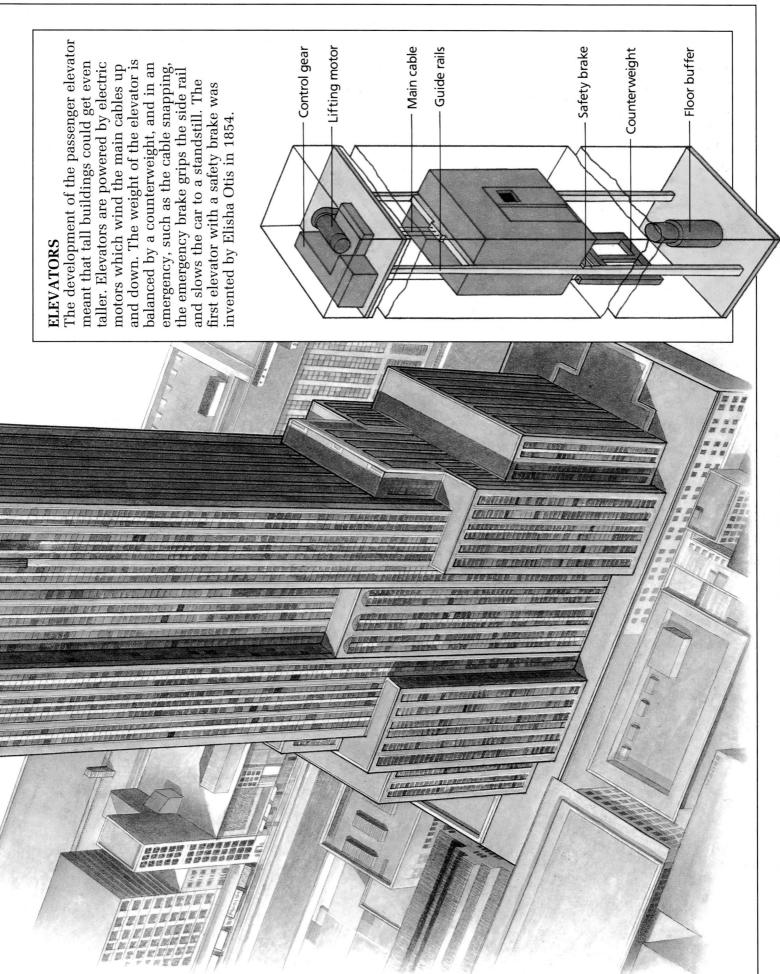

Control gear

Lifting motor

Main cable

Guide rails

Safety brake

Counterweight

Floor buffer

THE HOOVER DAM

People have always tried to dam rivers to change their courses or to collect water. In the 20th century another purpose has arisen—the generation of electricity. After 1902, the U.S. Bureau of Reclamation became the world's biggest builder of dams, as it built generating plants run on water power. In the late 1920s, the bureau undertook its greatest project, to dam the Colorado River in the Black Canyon, 25 miles from Las Vegas. The Boulder Dam (later renamed the Hoover Dam) has a greater volume than all of the bureau's 50 earlier-built dams put together.

THE HOOVER DAM

TYPES OF DAM

Until the mid-19th century, most dams consisted of **barrages** of compressed earth which tended to leak. The French were the first to evolve a design which was convex in plan, arching into the flow of the water. The first scientifically designed dam was the Furens Dam at Saint Etienne (1866). Since then, as this diagram shows, dams of many different types have been built. The biggest are earth-filled barrages like the Tarbela Dam in Pakistan.

TYPES OF DAM

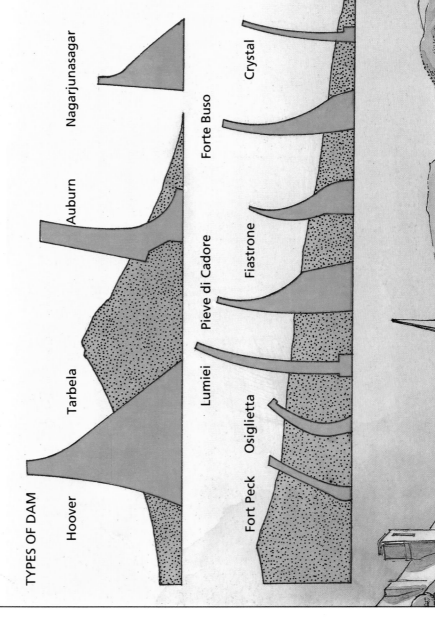

Hoover

Tarbela

Auburn

Nagarjunasagar

Forte Buso

Crystal

Pieve di Cadore

Fiastrone

Lumiei

Osiglietta

Fort Peck

LAYOUT

The Hoover Dam is a gravity-arch dam. The arch curves into the artificial lake formed so that the water pressure is against it, compressing the concrete arch into the rock cliffs.

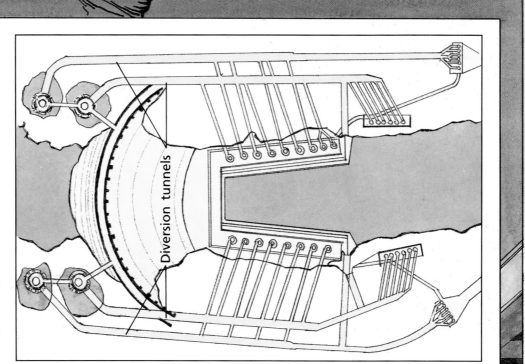

Diversion tunnels

THE WALL

At the base of the dam a U-shaped 400-foot-long powerhouse was constructed. The Hoover Dam created a lake, Lake Mead, behind it. It is 115 miles long and nearly 8 miles across at the widest point. In the powerhouse, 17 huge generators produce an electrical capacity of 1.3 million kilowatts.

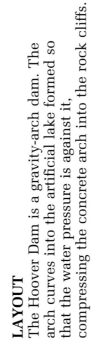

L'UNITE D'HABITATION

In the 1920s and 1930s, some architects developed the possibilities of building with reinforced concrete into a style later known as the modern movement. The most prominent, a Swiss named Le Corbusier, listed "Five Points of a New Architecture": 1. The building should be raised off the ground on vertical stilts, or **pilotis**. 2. The plan of the floors should be free, not bound by a rigid set of rooms. 3. The facade should be similarly free, and not load-bearing. 4. Windows should be horizontal strips within the facade. 5. The roof should be flat, allowing for a roof garden.

L'Unité d'Habitation, a large concrete apartment complex, displays all these points.

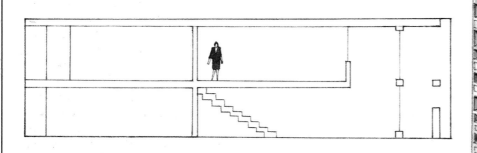

LIVING IN L'UNITE
The apartments are generally L-shaped in section, making them almost two-story. Every third floor a street runs across the building. The shopping street is halfway up the building.

VILLA SAVOYE
One of Le Corbusier's most famous houses is the Villa Savoye, near Paris. It incorporates all his "Five Points." How many can you see from the outside?

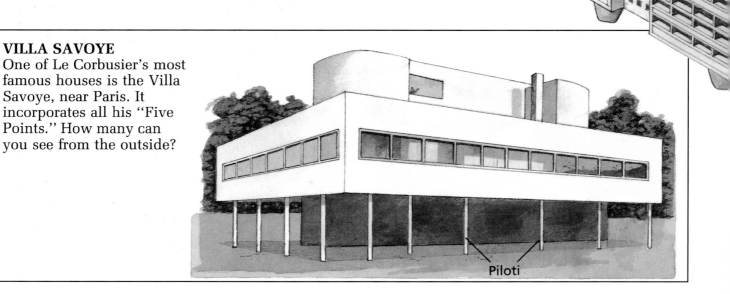

Piloti

CONCRETE

Modern concrete is a carefully controlled mixture of water, sand, cement, and aggregate (a coarse material, like gravel), which can be poured into a mold of virtually any shape. Nowadays, concrete in a building's structure is almost always reinforced by the addition of thin steel rods.

MODERN MOVEMENT

The modern movement architects were inspired by the American skyscrapers, and the designers of these, in turn, incorporated modern movement features into them. Le Corbusier said that a house should be "a machine for living in," and in the 1920s he designed several houses for wealthy clients near Paris. After World War II he had the opportunity to design a much bigger "machine for living in," the 18-story apartment complex known as L'Unité d'Habitation, in Marseilles.

PILOTIS

Raised on thick reinforced concrete pilotis, the Unité's reinforced concrete frame contains 337 maisonettes, or apartments, ranging in size from small units for only two people to much larger ones for families. Most importantly, the building also provides the community of 1,500 with a track, gymnasium, nursery school, hotel, restaurant, swimming pool, kindergarten, and grammar school on the top floor.

SYDNEY OPERA HOUSE

In 1957, a young Danish architect named Jørn Utzon won a competition to design an arts center in Sydney, Australia. The site was an exposed spit of land in Sydney Harbour named Bennelong Point. Utzon's design was a fantastic array of billowing white concrete sails enclosing a concert hall and an opera house. For the next 16 years engineers and builders sought to realize his vision. Work began quickly, and a vast concrete plinth, or base, was constructed over the whole of Bennelong Point, while plans for the shells, or roofs, were evolved. The precise shapes that Utzon had planned for were found to be impossible to build, but he discovered that with alterations building could proceed.

THE WINDOWS

The large walls of glass are supported on steel posts which run the height of the shells. Horizontal bronze bars hold the individual panes of glass in position. There are over 2000 panes and each is double thickness, bonded together using plastic. This smothered outside noise and lessened the chance of glass falling inward.

STRUCTURE

The original design was too complex to build, so the shells were eventually made from prefabricated concrete ribs, all with the same radius, to make construction easier. The ribs were attached with glue and steel rods.

THE CONCERT HALL

Tile cladding units

THE SYDNEY OPERA HOUSE

The great shells of the Sydney Opera House cover five halls, one each for opera, concerts, plays, chamber music, and exhibitions. The hall used for opera is actually smaller than the concert hall, so though the building is called the Opera House, it is not able to put on large-scale operas.

THE SYDNEY OPERA HOUSE

THE CLADDING
The bright white cladding on the shells is built up by more than 1,000,000 ceramic tiles, each about the size of an audio cassette. The tiles were made up into 36-foot by seven-foot sections, then bolted to the roof.

THE OPERA HALL

Precast units in position

TIMEFRAME AND COST
The Sydney Opera House was started in 1959 and finished in 1973, when it was opened to the public. While the cost was estimated at 7,000,000 Australian dollars (A$), the final cost was nearer A$102,000,000.

PREFABRICATION
Each of the shells was made from ribs which were prefabricated on the site. They curve inward, and where they meet they are joined by concrete. It took 2,194 ribs to complete the building.

TOWER CRANES
Tower cranes grow to great heights to reach the tops of tall buildings. The cab lifts itself on hydraulic jacks, hauls up a segment of material to the correct height, inserts it, comes back down, and repeats the operation.

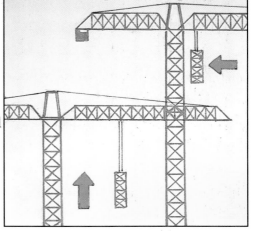

THE SAILS
The giant white sails look as if they are supported at two small points, but they are actually supported at four points. They are attached underneath to smaller shells, which keeps them from falling.

HABITAT, MONTREAL

The 20th century has seen widespread use of prefabrication using reinforced-concrete building components. Particularly following World War II (1939–45), mass housing has been put up all over the world. **Precast** walls, floors, and roofs have been assembled by different systems (hence the term "system building") into blocks of apartments. Many of these tower blocks are now condemned as ugly and inhuman, but not all are. Some were just badly designed. One of the most imaginative examples was the housing scheme called Habitat, designed by the architect Moshe Safdie for the Expo 67 International Exhibition in Montreal.

WAYS OF ASSEMBLY

The size of the basic module was fixed as that of a single-bedroom house which could also serve as half or one quarter of larger houses; the module size was 17 feet by 38 feet, with holes cast in for doors and windows. The modules could be arranged, like dominoes, into many shapes. These dominoes, though, weighed 77 tons each.

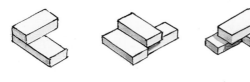

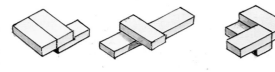

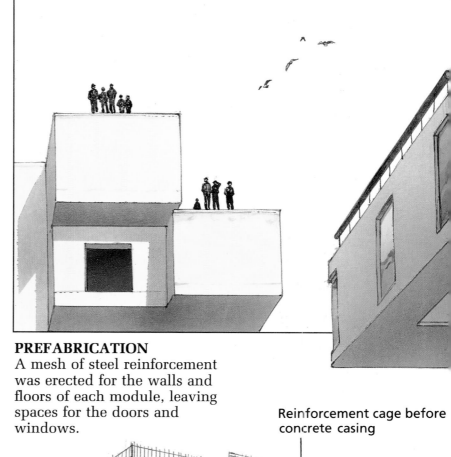

PREFABRICATION

A mesh of steel reinforcement was erected for the walls and floors of each module, leaving spaces for the doors and windows.

Reinforcement cage before concrete casing

HABITAT

The prefabrication process did not end with the walls of the modules—bathrooms and kitchens also came as complete units, with all the fittings in place. Think back to Le Corbusier's idea of a modern house being "a machine for living in." It is certainly logical for a machine to be assembled complete in a factory.

THE DESIGN

Safdie designed not just elements to be precast, but whole room units to be brought to the site complete and lifted by crane into the fantastic complex of different sized and shaped apartments.

LAYOUT

Habitat modules were tied together with steel rods that had previously been put under tension so that they would pull the modules together. Casting concrete with the reinforcement rods already under tension is called **prestressing**.

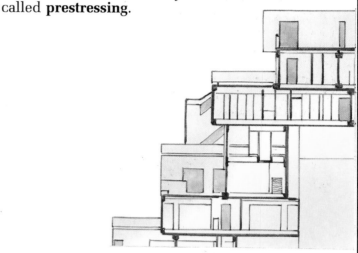

CONCRETING

Concrete was poured around the reinforcing mesh and left to dry and harden. When it was solid, the molds were lifted away from the module.

After concrete casing

BATHROOM UNITS

An average bathroom consists of about 500 separate pieces. Habitat's bathrooms came as one molded fiberglass unit that was lifted by crane into the finished module.

SYDNEY HARBOUR BRIDGE

The first examples of steel arch bridges (the Garabit Viaduct, for example) had the road above the arch. When Australia's Sydney Harbour was bridged, a different method of employing the arch principle was used. Rather than supporting the deck from beneath, this type of bridge has a strong arch which rises high above the harbor, with the road and railway deck suspended below from steel hangers. The previous 50 years had seen longer and longer steel arch spans being constructed, but Sydney Harbour Bridge—and New York's Bayonne Bridge, also built in the early 1930s—were huge leaps forward. Their spans were more than half again as long as the previous recordholders.

ANCHOR CABLES
Like the Garabit Viaduct, the two halves of the Sydney bridge were built out from each side as cantilevers, anchored back by wire cables. These held the growing sections firm as they grew outward toward each other. Just before the two halves of the bridge met, the anchor cables were holding the entire weight of the bridge, so the fixing points at each end had to be immensely strong to carry this load. The main arch members of the span were the heaviest pieces of steelwork ever constructed.

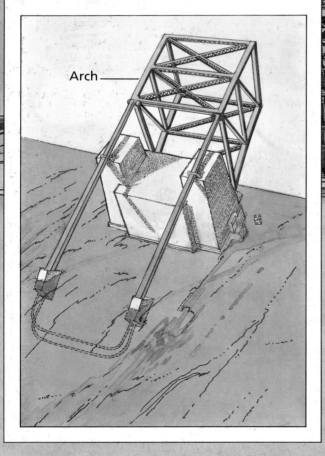

Arch

BAYONNE BRIDGE
The Bayonne Bridge, another steel arch bridge, is slightly longer, at 1,652 feet, compared with Sydney's 1,650 feet. But Sydney's is more massive.

THE ARCH
When they were within 3 feet of meeting, the wire cables were slackened off so that the two halves of the bridge sank toward each other and were joined.

STEEL STRUCTURE
The steel members, which had come from England, were built into sections in temporary workshops on the harbor side. These were floated out on the river, positioned under their place in the growing bridge-half, and then hoisted into place by the cranes which crept out from the shore on the growing ends of the cantilevered arches.

SYDNEY HARBOUR BRIDGE

Sydney Harbour Bridge carries two overhead electric train tracks plus eight highway lanes with sidewalks. Its total width is nearly 164 feet. No broader bridge has ever been erected. Seventy-two locomotives, each weighing 8,375 tons, were used to test the bridge for structural defects.

THE DECK

Once the arch was finished, the cranes were moved back, dropping the hangers and sections of suspended road and railway into place as they went.

GOLDEN GATE BRIDGE

During the 20th century the suspension bridge has become the clear winner in the race to span really long distances. The two cantilever spans of the Forth Bridge were still the world's longest at the turn of the century, and they were only marginally surpassed by Canada's Quebec Bridge in 1917 and Detroit's Ambassador Bridge in 1929. This last was a suspension bridge, however, and only two years later, New York City's George Washington Bridge nearly doubled the record span with its 3,500 feet. In 1937, even this was exceeded by San Francisco's Golden Gate Bridge, which at 4,200 feet held the record for nearly 30 years.

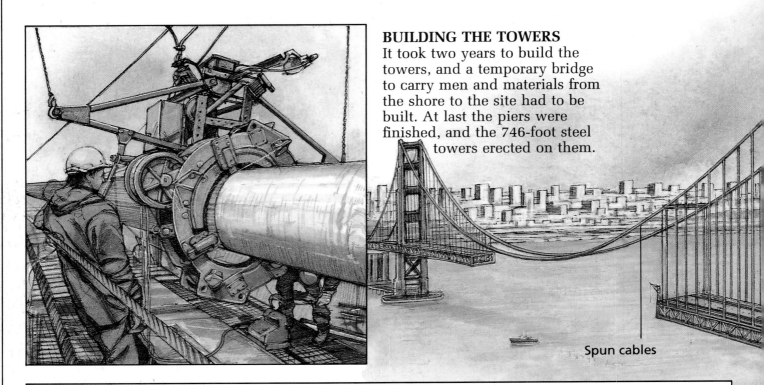

BUILDING THE TOWERS
It took two years to build the towers, and a temporary bridge to carry men and materials from the shore to the site had to be built. At last the piers were finished, and the 746-foot steel towers erected on them.

Spun cables

PLACING CABLES
To make the cables, 27,752 thin wires were spun back and forth across the gulf by continuously traveling wheels, 24 wires at a time. Each strand, formed by 450 wires, was clamped into the anchorages, or supports, at each end, and 61 of these strands were finally compacted into the cables, each over three feet thick. Over these the wire rope suspenders were hung, at 49-foot intervals, and these supported the deck sections.

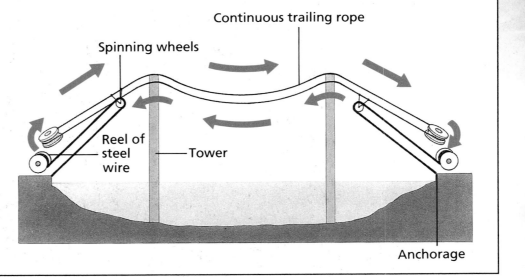

Continuous trailing rope

Spinning wheels

Reel of steel wire

Tower

Anchorage

GOLDEN GATE BRIDGE

The Golden Gate Bridge took six years to build. In the year of its opening, 1937, it was named Most Beautiful Steel Bridge by the American Institute of Steel Construction.

Steel tower

ROAD SECTIONS

The Golden Gate Bridge is very flexible: the towers can safely sway from the vertical 18 inches toward the channel or 22 inches shoreward. In high winds the roadway can deflect, or move, up to 28 feet side to side or 16 feet up and down.

THE PIERS

The north pier, built to carry the suspension tower, was supported quite easily on a rock ledge only 20 feet below the water, but the south pier had to be placed in over 100 feet of water, nearly 2,000 feet from the shore.

THE MODERN WORLD

Today, people have become aware of a conflict between the natural environment and the world we have built. Much of the natural environment has been spoiled and plundered. Trees are cut down for lumber, land is cleared and flattened for building, and quarries are dug for stone, cement, or sand. For nearly all the thousands of years we have been building, we do not seem to have worried about the effect of this on our planet. During this time we have acquired many skills without which we could not live as we do today, or at least enjoy what is called civilization. Unfortunately, some of these skills have had a negative impact on the environment. Some architects realize this and have designed buildings, such as those in this section, that attempt to reduce this impact.

THE POMPIDOU CENTER

In 1969, Richard Rogers and Renzo Piano won a competition to design a new cultural center in Paris. The building had to include a museum of modern art, a reference library, a center for industrial design, and a center for musical and acoustical research. The architects responded to the contest with a design which gave as much flexibility as possible—vast broad floor areas unencumbered by building services such as escalators, elevators, stairs, toilets, water supply, air conditioning, and electricity. What did the architects do with them? The answer was simple: they put them all on the outside of the building.

PUBLIC CENTER

Popularly called the Beaubourg, the Pompidou Center opened in 1977. Since then it has been used by tens of thousands of people per week. In terms of both public access and structure, the Crystal Palace's spirit was reborn 125 years later.

THE STRUCTURE

Each floor is divided into 13 bays, or areas, separated by the main structural elements, cast-steel trusses 150 feet long, 10 feet deep, and weighing 83 tons each. These were brought, three a week, in dead of night when there was no traffic, through the winter of 1974–75, and bolted to the main steel columns with 11 ton cast-steel joinings called gerberettes.

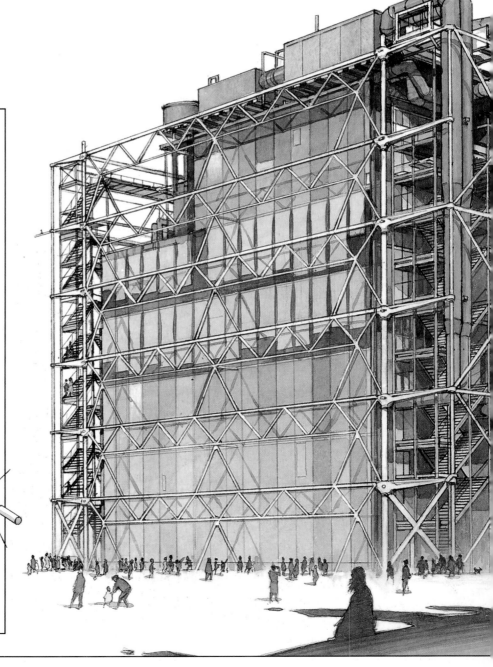

POMPIDOU CENTER

The rear is covered with huge colored ducts— green for water, blue for air conditioning, yellow for electricity, with red elevators plying up and down as well. At the front, escalators enclosed in transparent tubes snake upward from floor to floor, linking external walkways.

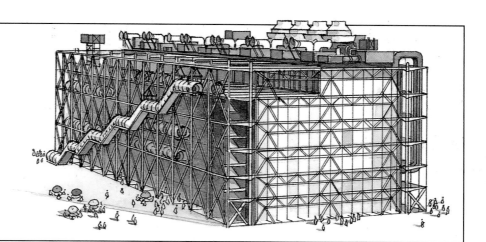

GLASS WALLS

The walls are glass, and beyond each floor on the escalator side is a 20-foot cantilevered platform containing the walkway.

SERVICE DUCTS

The design leaves all six floors free of building services—each floor 545 feet long, 157 feet wide, and 23 feet high, enough to allow the individual floors' service ducts to bring in electrical supplies and air conditioning over the people using the spaces, and out of the way of the museum exhibits.

OLYMPIC STADIUM

The problems in making large tentlike structures have been the low tensile strength of most tent materials and their tendency to flutter or billow in the wind. The latter problem can be overcome by introducing double curvature, or anchoring the material in two directions at 90° to each other. But this introduces very high tensile forces.

Pull the average tent really tight so that it doesn't flap, and the chances are that it will tear. This problem was overcome by introducing strong cables as the main structural elements. They are capable of withstanding the tension of being doubly curved and so can allow for a large tented building, as in Munich's Olympic Stadium.

The first important example of a doubly curved cable-net structure was the 328-foot-span Raleigh Arena, erected in North Carolina in 1952.

Supporting pylons

AFTER STRESSING
Some 130 miles of steel cable were needed to create the bolted-together square mesh of the cable net, prestressed for added tensile strength.

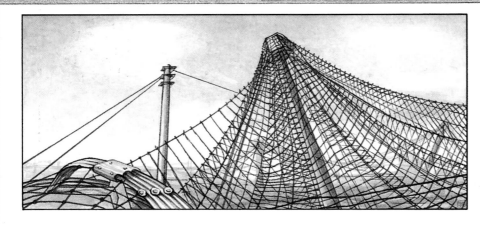

STEEL NETTING
All roof areas were supported from 56 pylons, or towers, and masts varying from between 23 feet and 260 feet high and anchored into concrete foundations at no fewer than 123 points around the outside.

OLYMPIC STADIUM

The size and complexity of the stadium resulted in many problems. No tensile roof of comparable size has since been attempted, although numerous smaller ones have provided lightweight and economical coverings to buildings of many different types in the years since construction of the Munich stadium.

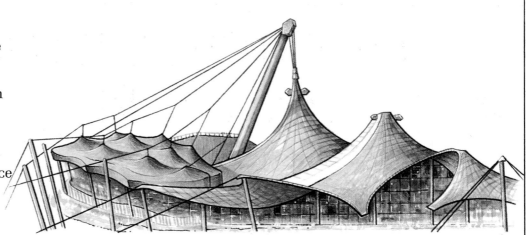

CERAMIC TILES

After much consideration, 8,500 transparent acrylic-glass panels were chosen for the roof skin itself, each one 10 feet square and about ⅛ inch thick, hung beneath the cable net.

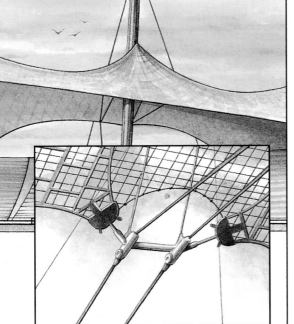

ANCHOR CABLES

The roof was held taut by thicker and stronger edge cables bolted to the main cables hanging the structure from the pylons, and more cables anchoring it to the ground.

COMPLEX LAYOUT

The tensile roof over the competing areas covered: 371,905 square feet over the stadium, 234,123 square feet above the gymnasium, and 128,095 square feet covering the swimming arena, plus an additional 71,044 square feet of linking areas.

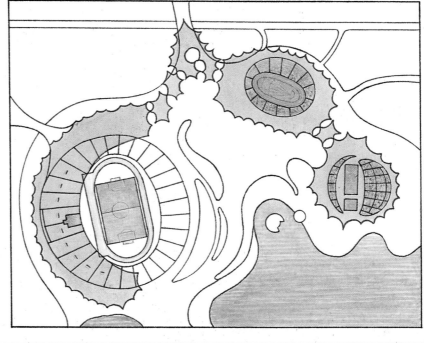

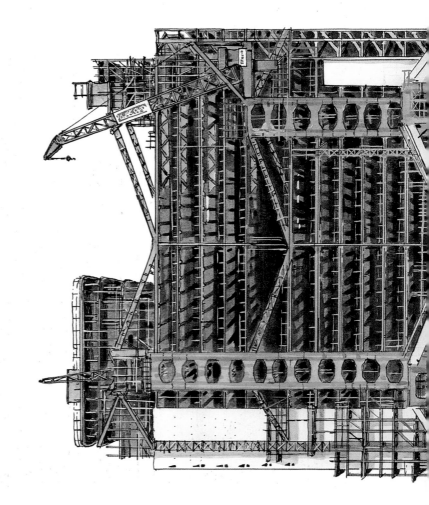

HONG KONG BANK

The new headquarters building of the Hong Kong and Shanghai Bank in Hong Kong was built between 1981 and 1985. It has been dubbed the most expensive office building in the world. Hong Kong is very crowded, so the architects, Foster Associates, had to design a skyscraper giving as much floor space as possible on a restricted site. "High-tech" means using new materials and building techniques—sometimes borrowed from civil engineering works like bridge design—and making a positive point of showing them off in the final appearance of the building. The floors of the Hong Kong Bank all hang from eight giant steel masts, each 656 feet tall.

SUNSCOOPS

In the atrium of the Hong Kong Bank, natural sunlight is ingeniously brought down from the top of the building by an arrangement of "sunscoops," or mirrors that capture the sunlight and reflect it downward.

HANGERS
The suspension trusses span 110 feet between the masts and project 35 feet beyond them. Tubular hangers drop down from the trusses, and the floors are suspended from these.

SUPPORT MASTS
The only supports at ground level are at the bottoms of the eight main masts, which allows for a sweeping, virtually uninterrupted entrance area. In the center of the building is a spectacular **atrium**— an open space several floors high (in this case, 11).

TRUSSES
Including the basements, the building has a total of 47 levels. The groups of floors hang from suspension trusses.

ATRIA
Atria, or large internal open spaces, have become fashionable in late 20th-century architecture, both in high-tech building and in postmodernism, a style which reacted against the purity of modernism by the deliberate inclusion of decoration.

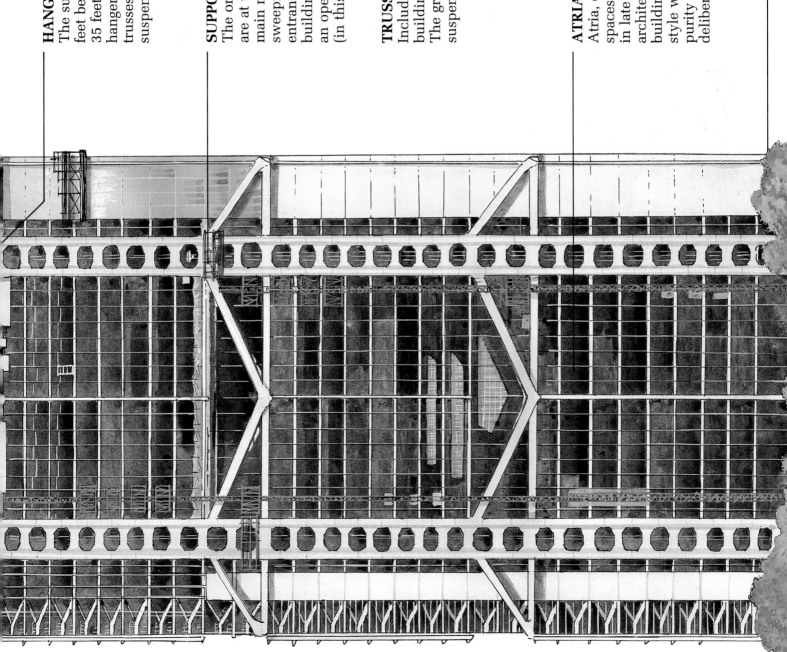

THE CHANNEL TUNNEL

A tunnel under the English Channel has been thought about for nearly 200 years. Since the beginning of the 19th century, England and France have planned to link their two countries with a tunnel. In 1802, one proposal saw horse-drawn carriages rumbling through a brick-lined passageway just below the sea-bed, while in 1880 work began on a tunnel, and two miles were actually dug before the project was abandoned. In the early 1970s, work began again at the same site, but for political reasons it was again halted. Finally, a train tunnel that could carry freight, passengers, and cars was proposed. Work began in 1987, with a planned opening date of 1993.

LASER MEASURING

It is very important that the tunnels follow the exact path that was planned for them. Each tunnel was designed to be dug outward from the shore, so if either end were off course, the ends would never meet. To prevent this from happening, the engineers use lasers which can very accurately measure distances and, because of their long, straight beams, indicate whether the tunnel is off course in any way.

THE CUTTER

The tunnel boring machine (TBM) has a rotating cutting head fitted with over 100 cutting rollers. To withstand the wear and tear, they are made from the metal tungsten.

CONVEYOR BELT

This conveyor belt carries the many tons of earth cut away by the cutting head. It passes the waste back to wagons, which transport it to the surface.

DRIVER

The cutting head, which rotates up to three times a minute, is powered by a large electric motor. The whole TBM is pushed forward by massive hydraulic rams and steered by smaller side rams.

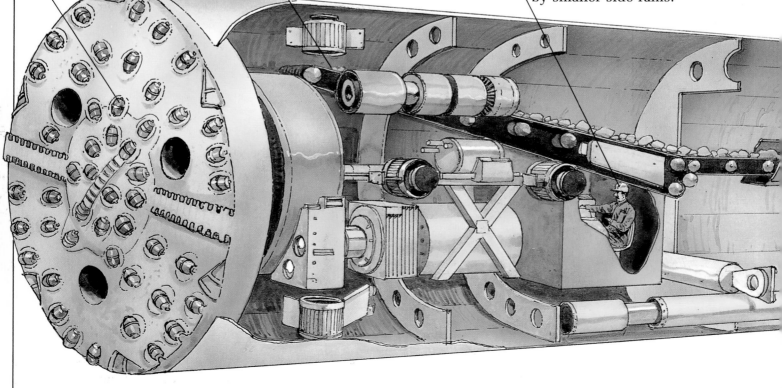

SANGATTE SHAFT

The tunnelers on the English side have entered the tunnel at ground level. The French have decided on another method. Their access point is a vast shaft sunk 213 feet into the ground. Within its 184-foot diameter are all the mechanisms for supplying everything needed at the face, or wall, that is being dug into, along with all the systems for removing the huge amount of earth that is cut away as the tunnel is dug. Giant elevators pass sections of tunnel lining down to wagons that will carry the lining to the face. Grout to seal the gaps between the lining slabs and waterproof the tunnel is made in large quantities on site.

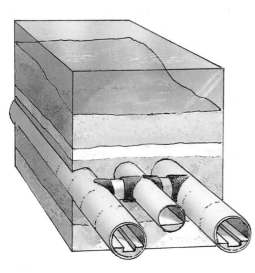

THE CHANNEL TUNNEL
The tunnel is actually made up of three separate tunnels. Trains run in two, and the central tunnel is a service shaft, linked to the main tunnels every 1,230 feet. The structure is between 56 and 131 feet below the seabed.

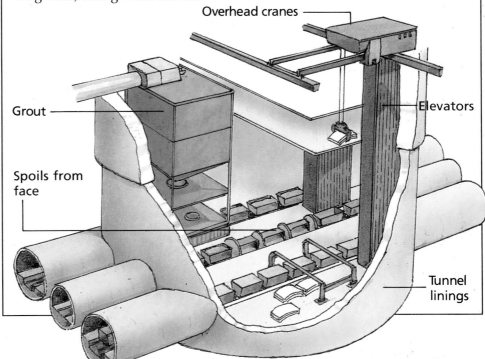

Overhead cranes

Grout

Spoils from face

Elevators

Tunnel linings

CLADDING
The tunnel lining, or cladding, is put in place in sections. These are passed to the workface along a conveyor belt from the mouth of the tunnel.

PERMANENT DECK
As the tunnel grows, a permanent, preformed floor is carried in and laid down.

VENTILATION
Large pipes carry air into the tunnel and take away unwanted gases.

GOODS IN
Materials need to be transported to the face quickly. Six wagons can carry enough to make two rings of tunnel lining.

A NEW BANK

From the late 19th century onward, our indoor environment has been controlled more and more by artificial means: gaslight was replaced by electric lighting; open fires were replaced by heating systems of various kinds designed to maintain constant indoor temperatures; air conditioning was invented to control temperature and the quality of the air that we breathe. But now all these things, regarded once as wholly beneficial, are seen as much less desirable. They all use up valuable energy and may contribute to global warming. The strange-looking buildings on these and the next few pages are all designed to be energy efficient.

THE ATRIUM
Natural sunlight also penetrates down each atrium, making it less necessary to use artificial light. The building has its own electricity generator, and the spare heat from this process is stored and used.

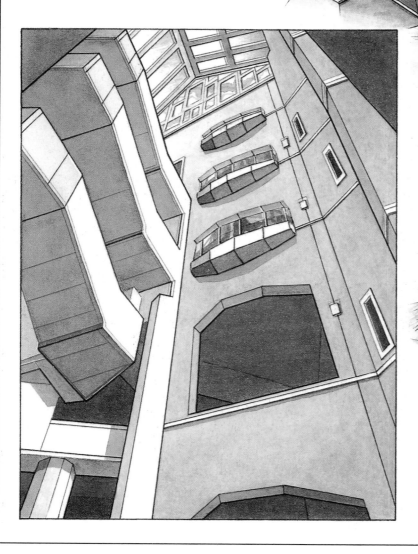

NMB BANK

The NMB Bank, in Amsterdam, Holland, is actually 10 buildings arranged very roughly into an S shape and joined by an internal street. Each building contains a cluster of offices grouped around a central atrium. On the top of each cluster are a five-sided array of solar panels that collect the sun's heat.

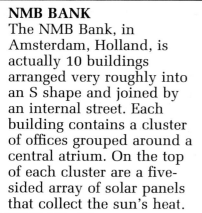

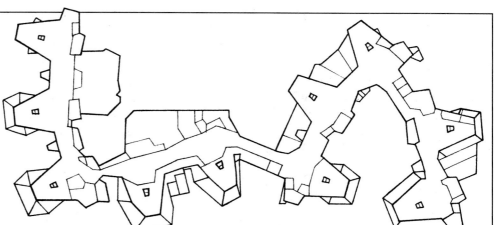

SOLAR PANELS

Even the sloping walls, which look so strange (but which are a little like some of those designed by Gaudí at the beginning of the century), assist with energy conservation, as does the apparently rambling ground plan. Both help to deflect wind and to maintain much of the building's heat.

ENERGY EFFICIENCY

Between the concrete structural walls and the outer sloping skins are 1.17-inch air gaps, which help keep heat inside during the winter. In the summer, cool streams of air flush through the building at night and carry away unwanted heat.

A NEW TOWN HALL

The energy-efficiency theme continues through another new building, still in the advanced-planning stage as this book is being written. It is the new county hall for the city of Marseilles, in France. Compare the architectural design with the NMB headquarters— though they are both very large buildings with floor areas totaling about 861,000 square feet,

they present a fascinating contrast. Compared to the organic, random appearance of the NMB Bank, the Marseilles county hall has a very high-tech appearance, with strips of floors carried on columns, atria between, and podlike top stories containing solar-energy collectors. This building also uses its **thermal mass** to store heat.

OUTSIDE PASSAGEWAYS
The corridors on the outside will act as buffer zones, lessening the effect of the outdoor climate. In the hot summer they will stop heat from getting to the office areas, and in winter they will insulate these same areas from the cold outside.

ENVIRONMENT SENSE
Around the world, people are realizing that it is up to us, as inhabitants of the Earth, to conserve energy and preserve our natural environment. This could mean great changes in how buildings are designed. Both of these buildings, like many others being designed now, use technology sensitively to provide environments that are more comfortable and user-friendly. Both buildings consume less energy than do many buildings of the past.

The concrete structure will retain warmth from inside during winter nights and radiate it back into the offices during the day. On summer nights, outdoor air will cool concrete slabs, and during the day these slabs will absorb unwanted heat generated by the building.

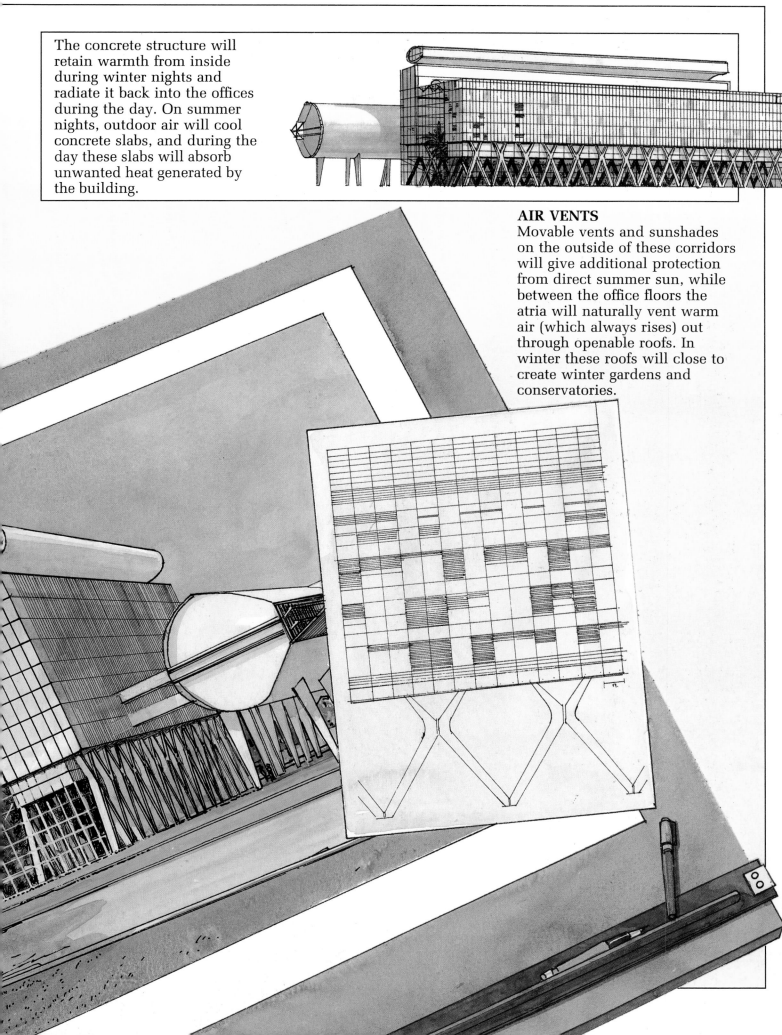

AIR VENTS

Movable vents and sunshades on the outside of these corridors will give additional protection from direct summer sun, while between the office floors the atria will naturally vent warm air (which always rises) out through openable roofs. In winter these roofs will close to create winter gardens and conservatories.

LA TOUR SANS FIN

At La Défense, the business region of Paris, one of the world's tallest buildings will be constructed in the early 1990s. The name literally means "the tower without end" – a modern Tower of Babel? The architect, Jean Nouvel, has designed an 80-story cylinder which will be narrower in relation to its height than is any other existing skyscraper. It will have a unique appearance—solid and dense, with relatively small windows near ground level. It will appear progressively lighter as it climbs, with the top 164 feet or so seemingly transparent.

SWAYING AND STRESSES

The top quarter will have a steel frame to further reduce the tendency to sway, while the final section, equal in depth to about 14 stories, as well as looking transparent from the ground, will have an open lattice structure designed specifically to counter pressures building up from high winds.

STUNNING VIEWS

Outside, the tower will have a very obvious spiraling, criss-cross pattern. Since the **structure** of the tower will be completely on the perimeter, or outside (unlike a steel frame or a central concrete core), the floors will be completely column-free, allowing stunning views out beyond the structural frame to the skyline of Paris.

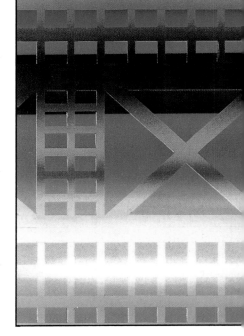

CONCRETE FRAME

Putting the structure at the perimeter of the tower was the only way to make such a slender building stable. Either steel or reinforced concrete would have been suitable, but the structure requires such a large amount of material that steel would have been too expensive. So concrete is being used.

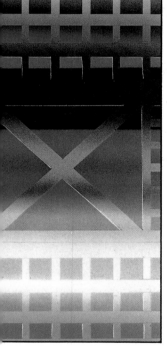

CROSS SECTION

The tower will be massive near the base and become lighter in appearance as it rises.

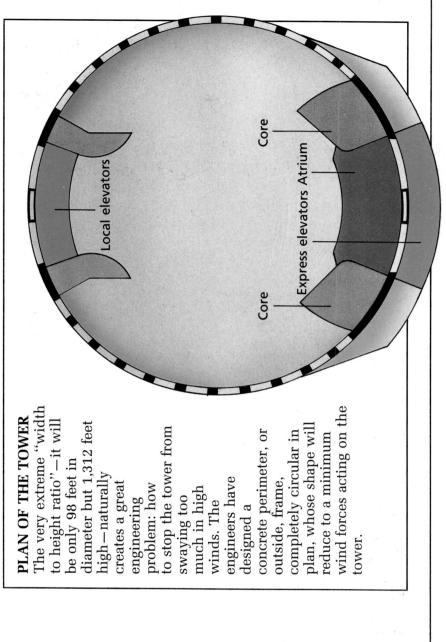

PLAN OF THE TOWER

The very extreme "width to height ratio"—it will be only 98 feet in diameter but 1,312 feet high—naturally creates a great engineering problem: how to stop the tower from swaying too much in high winds. The engineers have designed a concrete perimeter, or outside, frame, completely circular in plan, whose shape will reduce to a minimum wind forces acting on the tower.

KANSAI AIRPORT

Air travel has increasingly dominated the 20th century, and airports have grown to keep pace with it. Some, like London's Heathrow, have developed piecemeal over many years, but others have been planned completely from the start. Two miles offshore from the Japanese city of Osaka a whole artificial island is taking shape to house what will undoubtedly be the world's most spectacular and futuristic airport—Kansai International. Already complete is a two-level truss bridge for both trains and vehicles. It will carry some 25 million passengers a year back and forth from island to shore. Work has also begun on the central terminal building.

THE ARCHITECT
The architect is Renzo Piano, co-designer of the Pompidou Center in Paris. That was an extremely large and innovative building, but the Kansai terminal will be well over 10 times its length, from tip to tip of the two "wings" that extend outward on each side of the main passenger concourse.

CLEAR VIEW
At the front of the building, the roof wing will curve right down to ground level, wrapping around several floors and becoming a continuous glass wall through which passengers will have a clear view of the planes.

CROSS-SECTION
The intention is to have passengers arrive by train or car at the rear of the terminal and move more or less in a straight line toward their aircraft. This is very different from the confusing twists and turns of most airports.

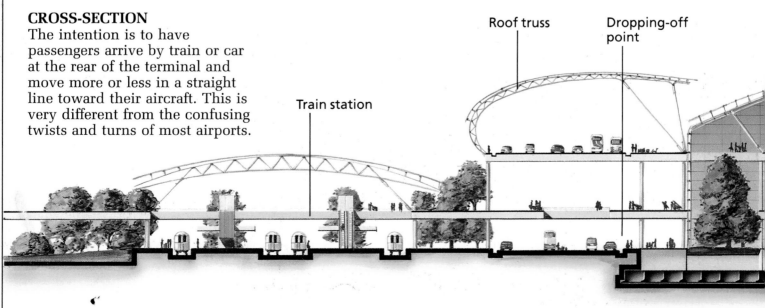

Train station

Roof truss

Dropping-off point

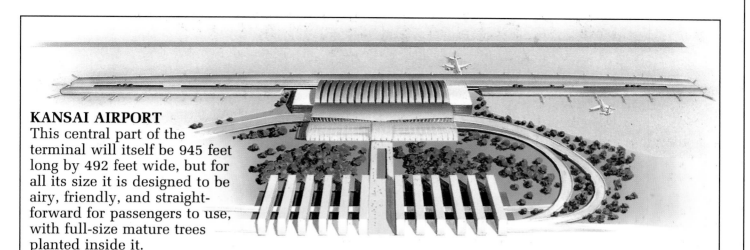

KANSAI AIRPORT

This central part of the terminal will itself be 945 feet long by 492 feet wide, but for all its size it is designed to be airy, friendly, and straight-forward for passengers to use, with full-size mature trees planted inside it.

THE DESIGN

The colossal roof will fly far over the heads of the passengers, and will be shaped like an airplane's wing section. It will be supported in bays along its length by three-dimensional trusses, the largest span between the raking support legs of these being as much as 272 feet.

ARCHITECT'S MODEL

Kansai International Airport is scheduled for completion in 1994, the year after England's Channel Tunnel will be completed. These are currently the world's two largest civil engineering projects, each in its own way presenting a vision of what 21st-century travel will be like.

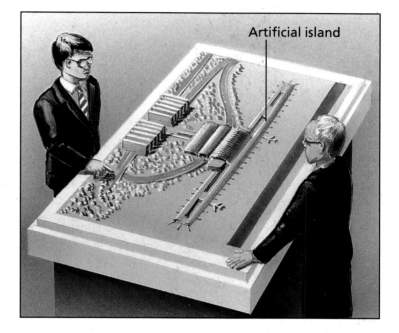

Artificial island

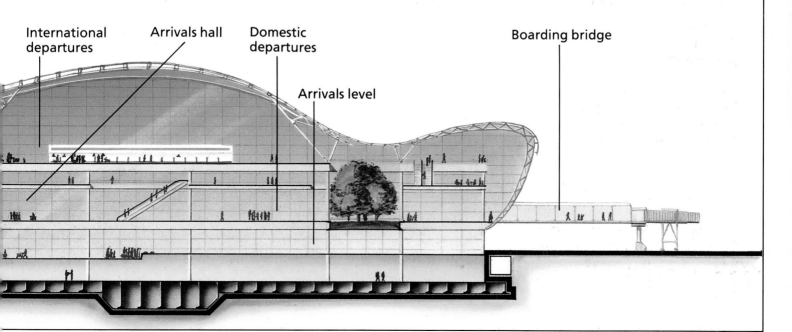

International departures

Arrivals hall

Domestic departures

Arrivals level

Boarding bridge

GLOSSARY

NOTE: If you see a word in italic type (*like this*), it means that you will find a definition of it somewhere else in the glossary.

Acoustics
The science of sound; the way sound is absorbed and reflected by the internal surfaces (walls, ceiling, floor, seats, etc.) of a room or hall.

Adobe
Sun-dried brick made of mud and often straw; sometimes a building made of such bricks.

Aqueduct
An artificial bridge or raised channel for carrying water, often over long distances.

Arch
A structure spanning an opening, usually curved, that can support its own weight.

Architect
A designer of buildings.

Architecture
The art and science of designing buildings.

Atrium
The main part of a Roman house; in late 20th-century *architecture*, an open space sometimes several stories high within a building.

Bailey
The outer wall or courtyard of a *medieval* castle.

Baroque
An ornamental style with a lot of decoration, sometimes very extravagant and flamboyant, that arose in the 17th and early 18th centuries. It can apply to *architecture*, art, and music.

Barrage
An artificial obstruction in a watercourse that increases water depth, facilitates irrigation, etc.

Barrel vault
A roof with a continuous semi-circular section.

Basilica
A Roman public hall and meeting place; its typical plan was later adapted for early Christian churches.

Beam
Any single horizontal (side-to-side) piece of a building's structure.

Buttress
A support, usually *masonry*, built against an outside wall (usually of a church) to give support.

Caisson
An enclosure built to keep the water out while the *foundations* of a bridge are being built.

Cantilever
A horizontal structural *member* securely fixed at one end and hanging freely at the other; a cantilever bridge has fixed arms, stretching out from an anchored base, supporting the central span between them.

Capital
The top part of a *column*.

Cast iron
A hard mixture of *iron*, carbon, and other elements, which melts easily and which can be poured into molds to form the *precast* parts of a structure.

Cement
A powder made by intense heating and then grinding of a mixture of *clay* and *limestone*, which with water turns sand and aggregate (sand, gravel, or slag) into hard *concrete*.

Centering
Temporary framework used to support a *masonry arch* while under construction.

Choir
The part of a church or cathedral occupied by the singers, opposite the *nave* on the other side of the *crossing*.

Circus
A circular or oval building or arena for games, particularly as built by the Romans.

Civil engineering
The design and construction of structures other than those we normally call buildings, such as roads, railways, dams, canals, bridges, docks, and harbors.

Classical
In *architecture*, the style of ancient Greece (and usually Rome); also, later work that imitates or uses parts of that style.

Clay
A type of earth, often pale in color; powdery when dry; solid, sticky, and workable when wet; one of the basic materials of *cement* and brick.

Cofferdam
A watertight enclosure from which water is pumped to expose the bottom of a body of water.

Colonnade
A row of *columns*, spaced at regular intervals.

Column
An upright structural *member*.

Concrete
A mixture usually of sand, *cement*, aggregate (sand, gravel, or slag), and water that is poured into formwork and hardens into a tough, stonelike building material.

Corbeling
Successive layers of *masonry* that project farther and farther beyond each other—either on two

sides, each pointing inward above an opening, usually meeting at the top; or singly at the edge of a building, to support a roof.

Corinthian
One of the ancient Greek *orders* of *architecture*, with a leafy style of decoration at the *capitals*.

Crossing
The space in a church where *nave*, *choir*, and *transepts* cross.

Cross vault
Two *vaults* meeting and crossing each other at right angles.

Cruck
Two pieces of naturally curving timber, usually cut from the same tree, pointing inward to support a primitive English house's roof, and forming part of the walls.

Crypt
A vault under the main floor of a church, usually containing graves or relics.

Dome
A large curved ceiling or roof, usually circular in plan.

Doric
One of the ancient Greek *orders* of *architecture*, with no decoration at the *capitals*.

Dressing
Cutting *stone* for building to its final shape.

Earthworks
A raised structure or other construction made of earth, often for fortification.

Facade
The (usually front) face of a building.

Facing
Outer layer of *stone* or brick on a building.

Flying buttress
Buttress built separately from a building; a sloping column of *masonry* curving upward to the wall to carry the weight from the *vault* down into the *buttress*.

Formwork
The timber or metal temporary form that "wet" concrete is poured into.

Forum
The marketplace or public square in an ancient Roman town.

Foundation
The base of a building or structure, usually below ground level, which carries the building's weight.

Frame
The skeleton of part or all of a building's structure, usually made up of *beams*, *columns*, and often braces.

Girder
Supporting *beam*, usually *iron* or *steel*, in a structure.

Gothic
In *architecture*, the style of building evolved in *medieval* times which developed the use of pointed, rather than semicircular, *arches* and *vaulting*.

Granite
A very hard, crystalline, usually speckled type of rock, which has solidified from the molten (liquid) state.

Groin
The curved edge formed where two *vaulting* surfaces meet.

Gutter
Channel for carrying away surface water.

Hammer beam
Short *cantilevered* timber supporting a wooden *arch*, often

found in church roofs, with decoratively carved ends.

H-beam
Beam, usually *iron* or *steel*, whose cross section is H-shaped.

I-Beam
Beam, usually *iron* or *steel*, whose cross section is I-shaped.

In situ
Building work, like casting *concrete*, done right at the structure's final location.

Ionic
Ancient Greek *order* of *architecture*, with scroll or spiral decoration at the *capitals*.

Iron
A hard metallic element, often processed in various ways (*cast iron, wrought iron, steel*) to form parts of buildings.

Joint
Any connection between two structural *members*.

Joist
A *beam* supporting flooring.

Keep
Fortress; the strongest part of a *medieval* castle.

Keystone
The central *stone* at the top of an *arch*, always put in last.

Kiln-fired brick
Brick baked hard in an oven, and more durable than sun-dried brick or *adobe* .

Lantern
Decorative construction, usually with glazing, at the crossing of a church or cathedral, often above a *dome*.

Lattice
Crisscross arrangement of structural parts.

Lead
Very heavy, soft metallic element, often used in thin sheets for covering church roofs.

Lever
A bar to which force is applied on the long end and transmitted to the short end by means of a block (fulcrum) placed under it.

Limestone
A type of rock, fairly easy to *dress*, composed mostly of calcium carbonate. Chalk is a very pure limestone.

Lintel
Beam above a doorway or window.

Load-bearing
Any part of a structure that is designed to carry the weight of other construction above it.

Marble
Hard *limestone* that has been recrystallized by intense heat; often colored, sometimes with very distinctive patterns; it can be shaped and polished to beautiful decorative effect.

Masonry
General term for building work in *stone*, and sometimes brick and *concrete* .

Mausoleum
A large and magnificent *tomb*, usually, but not always, ancient.

Medieval
A period of European history, roughly between the 11th and 16th centuries.

Member
Any unit of an *architectural* structure.

Minaret
A slender tower built above or near a *mosque*, and from which Muslim believers are called to prayer.

Moat
A deep, defensive trench outside a castle, often filled with water and spanned by a drawbridge.

Mortar
Material usually of *cement* and sand, often with lime, mixed with water, in which *masonry* is set.

Mortise
A slot or hole cut in a piece of wood or *masonry*, into which a *tenon*, on another piece, at right angles to the first, is inserted to form a *joint*.

Mosque
A Muslim religious building.

Motte
A mound on which a castle is built, surrounded by a *bailey*.

Mud brick
The simplest type of brick: blocks of *clay* shaped and often sun-dried; similar to and sometimes the same as *adobe*.

Nave
The main part of a church, where the congregation gathers; opposite the *choir*, on the other side of the *crossing*.

Orders
The styles of *classical architecture*, mostly defined by types of decoration at the *capitals*.

Parapet
A low wall placed to protect any spot where there is a sudden drop.

Pendentive
Triangular curved *vaulting* formed when a *dome* is cut into by supporting *arches*, and its top part removed.

Pile
Shaft of wood or *concrete* rammed or bored (or poured, if concrete) into the ground to form part of *foundations*.

Pilotis
Columns supporting an entire building, so that the whole ground floor space is free of walls.

Pinned joint
Any *joint* between *members* that allows them to rotate relative to each other (like the human knee).

Pisé de terre
Construction of whole walls *in situ* by ramming earth between *formwork*.

Pitched roof
Roof usually consisting of two slopes resting against each other.

Portico
Colonnade forming the entrance to a *classical* building.

Precast/Precasting
Casting of units, especially of *concrete*, away from the site; opposite of *in situ*.

Prefabrication
The making of any parts of a building or structure in advance, away from the site.

Prestress/Prestressing
Incorporation of cables or bars of very high *tensile strength* in *concrete*; these are *tensioned* either before or after the concrete has hardened, to strengthen it, as for *reinforced concrete*.

Pyramid
A solid with triangular sides meeting at a point; in ancient Egypt, funeral monuments with four sides, some of immense size.

Rafter
Inclined wooden roof *member*.

Reinforced concrete
Concrete strengthened by the inclusion of *steel* rods.

Rib
A band on a ceiling or *vault*, usually structural but sometimes decorative, separating the sections of a *groined vault*.

Ribbed vault
Vault with a band of *stone* forming an *arch* along the line of the *groin*.

Rivet
A bolt secured by hammering the end while hot so that it is clamped to the pieces being joined.

Romanesque
Pre-*Gothic* style of *architecture*, characterized by round *arches* and *vaults*.

Sandstone
Rock formed of compacted sand.

Sarsens
Large *sandstone* blocks found in south-central England, dressed and used in assembly and construction of Stonehenge.

Scaffolding
Temporary structure to support a building under construction and provide access for workers and materials.

Skyscraper
Very tall multistory office and/or apartment building, most often found in United States, but more frequently found worldwide since World War II; usually built to make fullest use of expensive sites in cities and towns.

Soffit
A ceiling; now, more usually, the underside of any structural *member*.

Spire
A tall, slender, *architectural* feature tapering to a point, usually on top of a church or cathedral tower.

Starling
In *civil engineering*, a pointed mass of *masonry* constructed in water to protect a bridge pier.

Steel
Compound of *iron* with less carbon than *cast iron*, but more than *wrought iron*; it combines the hardness (without the brittleness) of the first, with the workability of the second.

Stone
Naturally occurring rock; one of the oldest building materials.

Structure
Something, as a building or part of a building, that is constructed.

Stupa
A sacred Buddhist monument, usually an earth mound *faced* with brick and painted.

Suspension bridge
Bridge whose deck is supported from above by large cables suspended from towers.

Tenon
Projecting piece of wood or *masonry*, designed to form a *joint* by fitting into a *mortise* in another piece at right angles to it.

Tensile strength
The ability of a structural material to resist forces pulling it apart.

Tension
Force pulling outward on a *member*, usually from each end.

Terrace
A connected row of houses; a raised platform by a building; a series of shallow steps on which spectators sit or stand.

Thermal mass
The ability of a structure to absorb and retain heat.

Tomb
A monument in which the bodies of the dead are placed.

Tongue and groove
A joint made by a rib on one edge of a board fitting into a

corresponding depression on the edge of another board.

Transepts
The two parts of a church or cathedral at right angles to the *nave*, meeting at the crossing.

Truss
A *frame* of structural *members* capable of supporting weight over long spans.

Tympanum
The area between the *lintel* of a doorway and the arch above it; also, the triangular space enclosed by the moldings of a pediment.

Vault/vaulting
Arched covering, usually in *masonry*, over any part of a building.

Vice
A circular stairway inside a building.

Void
A gap or opening left within a wall, between a floor and ceiling, for example.

Wattle and daub
A *lattice* of thin twigs or branches (wattle) plastered with mud (daub) to make a crude building material.

Wrought iron
Almost pure *iron* with very little carbon, much softer than *steel* or *cast iron*, and easily worked.

Ziggurat
Ancient Mesopotamian *pyramidal* tower, usually of *kiln-fired bricks* facing sun-dried *mud bricks*.

INDEX

4/1 53 circ (3/05)